CANADIAN ANTI-COMBINES ADMINISTRATION
1952—1960

Canadian Anti-Combines Administration 1952-1960

G. ROSENBLUTH and

H. G. THORBURN

University of Toronto Press

Reprinted in 2018
ISBN 978-1-4875-7329-4 (paper)

Preface

Preface

IN MOST CANADIAN universities economics and political science
are joined together in the same department, but their union is
now purely formal. To an increasing extent the social scientist
must specialize, and it is becoming more and more difficult for
specialists in the different fields to talk to one another.

To some extent this trend is regrettable. The theory and practice
of public policy in economic matters are areas that cut across the
fields of academic specialization, and their study calls for the
skills of both the economist and the political scientist.

This essay is the result of collaboration between an economist
and a political scientist in the study of anti-combines policy and
administration. We focus our attention on the period between the
establishment of the present administrative machinery in 1952
and the recent major revisions in the definition of offences under
the Combines Investigation Act in 1960. We attempt to explain
the legislative innovations, and the manner in which the Combines Investigation Act has been administered, by reference to
the political and economic forces that influence the activities of
Canadian governments.

The object of our essay is therefore description and analysis, and not a search for the right policy. Certain recommendations do, however, emerge from the analysis, and these are summarized at the end of the final chapter. They are based on our view that the operation of the modern Canadian economy is improved by the promotion of free competition among business firms. The manuscript was completed in 1960 and our analysis does not deal with the administration of the act under the revisions of that year.

We wish to acknowledge the assistance of the former Director of Investigation and Research, Mr. T. D. Macdonald, and Messrs. Rhodes Smith and A. S. Whiteley of the Restrictive Trade Practices Commission, who provided information upon request. Mr. F. A. McGregor, Combines Investigation Commissioner before 1950, did likewise. Professors L. A. Skeoch, J. E. Hodgetts, and H. Scott Gordon read the manuscript and made many valuable suggestions. Mr. J. A. W. Gunn rendered capable research assistance.

Our work was aided by funds from Queen's University and the Canada Council. The Social Science Research Council provided a grant in aid of publication. For all this help we express our appreciation. The faults of the book are ours.

G. R.
H. G. T.

Contents

the committee's report: reorganization of the anti-combines machinery, the research function, and so on.

CANADIAN ANTI-COMBINES ADMINISTRATION
1952—1960

Introduction

Government plays a leading role in shaping the environment in which modern business operates. Taxes are a major component of business costs. Government buying provides a market, directly and indirectly, for numerous firms in a wide range of industries. Governments are expected to "do something" when recession threatens. Governments lay down and administer the rules under which private business firms carry on their activities. In Canada one of the most important means employed by the federal government to regulate business is the anti-combines machinery, which is intended to ensure that business activity remains competitive.

Although Canada was one of the first countries to legislate against combines, the extent of investigation and enforcement activity under this legislation has until recently been slight. It was not until 1948 that total expenditure for this purpose exceeded $100,000; now it is about $400,000. If "statutes live by appropriations," the Combines Investigation Act has only in the last decade recovered from prolonged privation.

Substantial increases in the scale of expenditures for combines investigation followed a major revision of the legislation and the administrative machinery in 1952. In this study we shall examine the circumstances surrounding this revision and the manner in which the combines machinery worked until it was again over-hauled in 1960. What were the forces making for change? Did the results justify the expectations? We shall conclude with a brief evaluation of the act as it worked up to 1960 and a summary of the revisions made in that year. It is too soon to offer comment on the operation of the machinery since this recent "revamping."

It is, of course, not to be expected that the legislative changes of 1952 can be explained in terms of a single force or a single set of co-ordinated objectives. Most major pieces of legislation are the results of compromise; compromise between the interests of different groups outside the government, and often also com-promise between different administrative and political objectives or even different forces within the cabinet. Combines legislation, being one of the most controversial areas of government policy, is particularly open to the impact of conflicting views and forces.

1. The Combines Act before 1949

THE RECOMMENDATIONS OF a parliamentary committee in 1889 were followed by legislation which, as amended in 1900, now stands as sub-section 1 of section 32 of the Combines Investigation Act. This makes it a crime to limit "unduly" trade, production, transportation, storage, and so forth, of goods or to lessen competition "unduly." Only in 1910, however, was administrative machinery set up for looking into alleged combines. Six citizens could apply to a judge, who would issue an order. The minister of labour would then appoint a board to investigate, and its report would be published in the Canada *Gazette*. This arrangement reflected the views of Mr. Mackenzie King, who felt that publicity rather than prosecution would be the most effective instrument in restraining illegal combines.

The act of 1910 proved ineffective, as there was no permanent machinery to enforce it and citizens were reluctant to come forward and lodge complaints. After an abortive experiment with a regulatory board (1919), Parliament enacted new legislation in 1923 which forms the basis of the present Combines Investigation Act. The act made it illegal to lessen competition by agreement, merger, or other means, where this was likely to operate to the detriment of the public. It provided for a permanent registrar, who made preliminary inquiries which could lead to a formal investigation either by the registrar himself or by a special commissioner. The resulting report was to be submitted to the minister of labour and was usually published. If it was a commissioner's report publication was compulsory, unless the commissioner himself advised against publication, in which case the minister could use his discretion.

After a second unsuccessful Conservative experiment with an administrative tribunal (1935), the Liberals in 1937 returned to the pattern laid down in the act of 1923. The registrar was transformed into a commissioner with the power to enter premises and seize documents, and the provision for the compulsory publication of reports was extended to those of the permanent commissioner. Some important investigations were conducted before the war broke out.[1] During the war, however, the government felt that the success of the controls over production, allocation, and prices depended on the support of business and on co-operation and consultation among firms. Accordingly, the government promised that no business practices pursued in the implementation of wartime controls would be attacked under the anti-combines legislation.[2]

The war thus constitutes an interregnum in the enforcement of anti-combines policies, and it also divides two periods which differ greatly in the nature and degree of enforcement. Before the war the commissioner had to make do with next to no staff. Expenditure for the earlier period was at its maximum in 1940, when $62,000 was spent. However, $38,000 of this represented legal fees, leaving only $24,000 to cover the activities of the commissioner. He never had more than one or two professional assistants and some clerical staff during this period. From 1923 to 1940 only twenty reports were made and sixteen published — one per year, on the average.

[1] For an account of pre-war legislation and activity under the act, see L. G. Reynolds, *The Control of Competition in Canada* (Cambridge, 1940), ch. vii.

[2] See Mr. Howe's statement in *Canada, House of Commons Debates*, Second Session, 1949, p. 1,500.

The evidence suggests that after the war combines investigation activity proceeded with somewhat greater vigour than in the thirties. Between the end of the war and 1949, seven reports were published. This was an average annual rate about twice as high as before the war. In addition a number of important investigations were launched that led to reports after 1949. Expenditures rose every year, to a peak of $169,000 in 1949, of which $65,000 represented fees and $86,000 salaries. Moreover, the list of topics and industries investigated suggests a more active policy. Of the pre-war reports, four dealt with the distribution of fruits and vegetables, seven with the distribution of coal, drugs, films, gasoline, and tobacco, two with building contractors, and only seven with combines among manufacturers, the products involved being bread, fruit baskets, radio tubes, tobacco products, rubber footwear, and paperboard containers. After the war a study of international cartels in manufacturing was followed by reports on combines in the manufacture of matches, glass, dental supplies, optical goods, bread, and flour. Large manufacturing firms were thus much more conspicuous among those investigated than before the war.

The coming of peace also saw the strengthening of the anti-combines machinery by amendments to the legislation. The administration of the act was transferred from the minister of labour to the minister of justice in 1945. An amendment passed in 1946 "restored to the Act a provision enabling the Commissioner to proceed on his own initiative with an inquiry to determine whether a combine exists or is being formed. A similar provision had been contained in the legislation from 1923 to 1937."[3] The act was further amended to provide for the appointment of deputy commissioners and to give the commissioner explicitly the power "to compile information and make studies concerning the existence in Canada of monopolistic conditions."[4]

Amendments passed in 1949 were designed to facilitate prosecutions. One of these "reaffirms, in effect, the principle that documents found in the possession of individuals are admissible

[3] *Annual Report of Proceedings under the Combines Investigation Act*, 1947, p. 3.

[4] 10 Geo. VI, c. 44, s. 3, An Act to Amend the Combines Investigation Act.

in evidence against them and extends it clearly to companies and unincorporated businesses which act through servants and employees." [5] This amendment was necessitated by the judicial decision in the Dental Supplies case, in which the defendants were acquitted on the ground that it had not been proven that the actions of company officers had been authorized by their firms. Other amendments provided that in combines prosecutions corporations should not have the option of trial by jury, and that the attorney-general of Canada (not only the attorney-general of a province) may institute and conduct combines cases.

Combines administration before 1949 contained paradoxical features which suggested the importance of compromise in administration. Mr. King showed concern about the combines problem and relied on publicity as the most effective weapon to curb excesses. In 1923 he asked: "What is the power of the criminal code to prosecute some particular person or group of persons in comparison with the power of spreading broadcast throughout the land accurate and true information with regard to a situation which is inimical to the public interest, and which the people themselves are certain to be concerned in remedying?"[6]

The commissioner or special commissioner who investigated an alleged combine had extensive powers to enter premises, seize documents, and order the attendance of witnesses to testify under oath. He then issued a report of his findings, which the law required to be published within fifteen days, whether the government found it agreeable or not, and regardless of any decision on the question of prosecuting the offenders in the courts. While the commissioner could not order business firms to change their practices or their structure (this could only be done through the courts), the compulsory publicity was intended to have a punitive effect, and fear of publicity was expected to keep firms from interfering with competition. Thus there was substance in the charge, often made by business interests, that the commissioner combined the functions of prosecutor and judge. In fact he acted as detective, prosecutor, judge, and then carried out the sentence (by publishing the report).

[5] *Report of the Commissioner of the Combines Investigation Act, 1950*, p. 2.
[6] *House of Commons Debates*, Second Session, 1923, p. 2625.

On the other hand the anti-combines administration was continuously starved for funds and consisted of a minimum staff. No economists trained to the Ph.D. level were employed in it prior to 1949. No market analysis or other economic research was involved in the reports, and no special research studies were launched. The commissioner was viewed as a watchdog to remain alert for infractions of the law. It was a police function carried on with a minimum of resources and, probably, with a minimal impact on business structure and practices.

Immediately after the war the Liberal party's platform included opposition to combines. The role of monopolies and international cartels in the development of Nazi power was widely publicized, and the Commissioner, Mr. F. A. McGregor, was encouraged to pursue his investigation of international cartels as well as his work on a United Nations commission dealing with this subject. In 1946, amendments strengthening the act, as well as increases in staff, followed recommendations contained in the Report on International Cartels.

The available evidence suggests that a change in policy took place during the St. Laurent-Howe administration. Proposals were made in the Cabinet to weaken the act, and in particular to reduce the concentration of power in the hands of the commissioner. The evidence on this point is connected with the Flour Milling case and is discussed in the next chapter.

2. The Flour Milling Report

The revision of the Combines Investigation Act, which established the present machinery, followed in large part the recommendations of the MacQuarrie Committee. This committee was appointed because of criticism of the government's administration of the act, especially the government's handling of the report on combines in the flour milling industry. The resignation of the Commissioner, Mr. F. A. McGregor, resulted from the treatment accorded the report, and it is worth while reviewing in some detail the events connected with Mr. McGregor's resignation.

Mr. McGregor began an investigation of the flour milling industry in September 1947 and forwarded his report to the Minister of Justice in December 1948. The conclusion of his investigation, presented with the supporting evidence in the report, was that the leading milling companies had maintained price fixing agreements "since at least 1936," through their trade associations in eastern and western Canada. These agreements were maintained in force during the war, and the firms were in collusion in bidding for government contracts.

Although the legislation in force at the time required the report to be published within fifteen days of its receipt, it was not tabled in the House of Commons for eleven months (November 1949, after McGregor's resignation) and was printed somewhat later. It was never distributed through the usual channels.

Mr. McGregor stated the reasons for his resignation in a memorandum attached to his letter of resignation, dated October 29, 1949, as follows:

First and foremost is my deep concern about certain tendencies that have been apparent in recent months which in my opinion seriously threaten the usefulness of this legislation.

One of the principal remedial measures provided by the Combines Investigation Act is the publication of reports of investigations. The withholding for so many months of publication of a report which the act requires shall be made public as soon as possible after its receipt (this is the only instance of the kind in my experience) is one illustration of the tendencies I have in mind.

Closely related to this are the differences of opinion on basic policy that have been revealed in our recent discussion relating to the flour investigation.... You have expressed the opinion that the inquiry should never have been started. I am satisfied in my own mind that the facts disclosed in the report more than justify the investigation.

... The investigation was started with the knowledge and approval of the then Minister of Justice, Right Hon. J. L. Ilsley....

I recognize fully that the making of policy is not the responsibility of a civil servant, but as a civil servant I would prefer not to carry on under conditions of uncertainty and conflicting tendencies such as I have experienced recently.

There is a greater need now for strong action under the Combines Act than there has been at any time in the past twenty-five years. To an alarming degree price fixing activities such as are reported in the flour milling industry have been developing in the post-war years; some of them originated in the war period, and some were started, as in the flour milling industry, even in the prewar years. To meet the situation ... the powers of the Combines Act should be strengthened. Council accepted in the present bill our proposals of three amendments, including a very important amendment designed to meet the difficulties of the dental judgment, but the only suggestions from Council which you called on me to consider seriously were provisions which would have had the result of limiting the effectiveness of the legislation. I have in mind such proposals as those to eliminate the Commissioner's initiative in launching inquiries, to place serious limitation on the requirements that reports be made public, and to provide for exemption, after prior approval, of certain types of agreements, to restrict production or eliminate price competition. These suggestions have not been included in the present bill, but my understanding from you is that consideration of them has been merely postponed pending a proposed "overhauling" of the act.... I am apprehensive ... particularly in view of the nature of the changes which have been suggested for consideration, of the ultimate result of any revision of the statute which would include changes along these or similar lines.

My hope is that my successor, in carrying out responsibilities which have many quasi-judicial aspects and call for a substantial measure of independent action and judgment, will have the support of an even stronger statute than the act in its present form, and a clear statement of government policy with respect to its enforcement.[1]

It should be pointed out that none of the suggested changes mentioned in this memorandum was really new. There is a long history of business opposition to the Combines Act, and the modifications mentioned had been frequently urged. They had, in fact, been included in the legislation that was in force from 1935 to 1937, and the commissioner's initiative in launching investigations was not restored until 1946.

After repeated enquiries by the opposition, the flour milling report was at last tabled in the House of Commons on November 7.[2] A debate took place which Mr. Howe opened for the government, although Mr. Garson was the responsible minister. He stated his objections to the portions of the report dealing with

---

[1] *House of Commons Debates*, Second Session, 1949, pp. 1516-17.

[2] Mr. Howe's leading role in this incident is also illustrated by the following exchange (*House of Commons Debates*, 1949, p. 1437):

Mr. Coldwell: ... the minister has tabled the letters in this case. Could they be printed in *Hansard* so that house members might have access to them?

Mr. Howe: Oh, no.

Mr. Garson: I would have no objection to that if it meets with ....

Mr. Howe: No.

Mr. Coldwell: Do we understand that all the correspondence is to be printed?

Mr. Howe: No, the custom is to table letters of resignation ....

Mr. Coldwell: Will they be printed in *Hansard*?

Mr. Howe: No.

the war and "decontrol" periods: "I was amazed to find that the flour milling industry was being condemned for carrying out policies that were obviously those of the Wartime Prices and Trade Board and those common to all control administrations."[3] He quoted a memorandum from Donald Gordon, former chairman of the Wartime Prices and Trade Board, in which the latter stated that under wartime controls and in the post-war decontrol period it was impossible to distinguish agreements leading to "combines" from those forming part of the system of government supervision. "For this reason, with the full knowledge of the Minister of Finance and of Mr. McGregor, I gave, as chairman of the Wartime Prices and Trade Board, orally and in writing, personal and repeated assurances that anything done in furtherance of the substance of the policy and administrative practices of the Wartime Prices and Trade Board would be held privileged."[4]

Mr. Howe made it clear that it was he who had urged Mr. Garson "not to table the report without further investigation."[5] "The full authority of the whole cabinet," however, supported the delay in tabling the publication. Mr. Howe concluded by stating his support for the Combines Investigation Act.

Opposition speakers, starting with Mr. Diefenbaker, were highly critical of the government's failure to abide by the Combines Investigation Act and publish the report. Mr. Diefenbaker suggested that the real reason for delay was that an election campaign was in the offing at the beginning of 1949. He also hinted that the government was not whole-hearted in its support of anti-combines legislation. "A law can be full of teeth, but if the teeth are not used to bite with it becomes a mere sham on the statute books."[6] While strongly criticizing the government's failure to comply with the law, he also repeated his earlier suggestion that the publication of reports before trial was "unfair."

C.C.F. and Social Credit speakers also deplored the government's action. Angus McInnis suggested that the delay in publi-

---

[3] *House of Commons Debates,* Second Session, 1949, p. 1500.
[4] *Ibid.,* p. 1501.
[5] *Ibid.,* p. 1500.
[6] *Ibid.,* p. 1506.

cation may have been intended to provoke Mr. McGregor's resignation.

The statements by Mr. Howe and other government spokesmen in this debate suggest that the government had come to regard combines as useful administrative devices. As Minister of Munitions and Supply, Mr. Howe had found that concentrated and collusive industries could be administered more easily than those involving a large number of competing firms, and his speech indicates that he did not consider it possible (or perhaps merely not desirable) to make a distinction between those collusive practices that were necessary for the smooth operation of controls and those that were not. It is a reasonable assumption that if Mr. Howe had considered the suppression of combines to be a matter of major importance he would have paid more attention to this distinction, or at least to the question whether it could be made in practice.

The government also objected to passages in the report dealing with the post-war period. Mr. McGregor had found evidence of a collusive price increase in September 1947, following removal of price control. Government spokesmen in the debate pointed out that the concerted action was taken at the suggestion of the government. Fearing still greater price increases following decontrol, government officials called a meeting of the leading millers' representatives and negotiated a price increase that was not to be exceeded, under threat of reimposition of the controls. Government officials were naturally indignant that concerted action with such a worthy aim and with the blessing of the government should have become the object of censure.

The administrative technique of persuading firms to agree to government suggestions, on the basis of the implicit or explicit threat of the use of administrative powers, is familiar from the field of banking, where it is known as "moral suasion." We do not know whether it was used in other industries besides flour milling in the inflationary period following decontrol, but the significant point is that its success depended on the existence of fairly high concentration and collusion among the firms concerned. If a government tries to fight inflation by persuading firms not to raise their prices, elements of monopoly and collusion in the economy are a great help. The government must, therefore, have lacked enthusiasm for the activities of the Combines Commissioner, who had repeatedly stated his convinction that the major danger to be fought by the anti-combines machinery was the persistence into the post-war period of the techniques and habits of co-operation acquired and strengthened in the war.[7]

In addition, the conflict over the publication of the flour milling report made it plain that the great concentration of powers in the hands of the commissioner could seriously embarrass the government if his views conflicted with government policy. The parliamentary debate indicates that strenuous efforts were made to induce Mr. McGregor to withdraw his report or to eliminate the sections to which the government objected. He refused to make any significant alterations, and his resignation, followed by parliamentary airing of the affair, gave a great deal of political ammunition to the opposition parties. It is hardly to be doubted that the government would wish to eliminate the possibility of such a situation arising again.

A review of the incident strongly suggests that a powerful group in the Cabinet favoured a reduction of the effectiveness of anti-combines activity and in particular a reduction of the powers of the commissioner. Mr. Howe seems to have been a leading member of this group. If such views were held under Mackenzie King, as they probably were, they were contained by Mr. King's support for the combines machinery, which was largely his creation, and his personal backing of Mr. McGregor, who had been his private secretary and was later to become his literary executor.

Cabinet proposals to weaken the effectiveness of the act are revealed in Mr. McGregor's memorandum cited above, and the fact that these proposals were made is confirmed by Mr. Garson in the debate. While little evidentiary value should be attached to the statements of opposition speakers, it is significant that they appeared convinced of the government's lack of enthusiasm for anti-combines activities. Finally, the whole handling of the

---

[7] See the Commissioner's annual reports, his memorandum of resignation quoted above, and his evidence before the Royal Commission on Prices.

flour milling report shows that any interest the government may have had in the suppression of combines was very easily overridden by other considerations. The government violated legislation enacted by the party then in power in order to protect a combine. While the legal aspects of this action are serious enough, its political significance can only be fully appreciated if one recalls that the publication of reports was something of a sacred cow in the King tradition of anti-combines procedure.

The Howe-McGregor conflict was sharpened by the fact that both of them viewed combines procedure as a matter of exposing "sin" (that is, infractions of the law), and not as a matter of studying and correcting structural defects in the operation of the economic system. Hence Mr. Howe felt very strongly, if one may judge by his remarks in Parliament, that any mention of non-competitive arrangements in the flour milling industry in a combines report was damaging to the good name of the firms concerned. This, he felt, was unfair since he himself considered these arrangements necessary and desirable.

Mr. McGregor's attitude is quite apparent from the combines reports that he wrote, as well as from his annual reports. It may perhaps be traced to Mackenzie King's notion that, while the concentration of business in large firms was inevitable, there could be little doubt about what constituted "good" and "bad" business behaviour, and the combines machinery was intended to ensure that business firms behaved themselves.

It seems most likely that after the flour milling incident the Cabinet was anxious to replace Mr. McGregor by a commissioner less strongly endowed with a sense of mission in his pursuit of combines and more amenable to direction from the Cabinet. They must also have favoured legislation to curtail the powers of the commissioner — in particular, his independence, and his powers of initiative and publication. The changes that were actually made must be viewed in the light of these probable aims.

3. The MacQuarrie Committee

THE POLITICAL PROBLEM facing the government after the parliamentary uproar over the flour milling report was how to obliterate the stigma of opposition to the investigation of combines, with which the opposition parties tried to brand it, and at the same time to introduce the modifications it considered necessary in the act. The traditional Canadian solution for such an impasse is the appointment of a royal commission. In this case the government appointed "A Committee to Study Combines Legislation" (not actually a royal commission), composed of Mr. Justice J. H. MacQuarrie of the Supreme Court of Nova Scotia; W. A. Mackintosh, Principal of Queen's University; G. F. Curtis, Dean of Law, University of British Columbia; and Maurice Lamontagne, a Laval University economist. The terms of reference of the committee were broad: "to study, in the light of present day conditions, the purposes and methods of the Combines Investigation Act and related Canadian statutes, and the legislation and procedures of other countries, in so far as the latter appear likely to afford assistance, and to recommend what amendments, if any, should be made in our Canadian legislation in order to make it a more effective instrument for the encouraging and safeguarding of our free economy." In addition, the committee was specifically asked to study the question of resale price maintenance.[1]

Business, agriculture, and labour expressed views before the committee. The submissions of business were the most numerous, since many general business organizations, trade associations, and even individual firms submitted briefs; despite their number, they all took the same general line.

The major complaint of the business briefs was directed at the "uncertainties" in the act. They objected to the terms "undue," "unreasonable," "likely to operate to the detriment of the public," and also to the uncertainty as to whether an accused party would be prosecuted under the Combines Investigation Act or the Criminal Code.

While attacking "uncertainty," most business briefs favoured a proposal which in practice would have increased the uncertainty in the administration of the act. They attacked the established practice of the courts in holding that the reduction of competition through a price agreement constituted "public detriment" in combines cases, and they urged that the Crown should have to show *specific detriment* in each case. Some, moreover, suggested that the word "likely" in the phrase quoted above should be replaced by "intended."[2] A brief by Mr. R. M. Fowler suggested: (1) that the statute should specifically list the permitted and prohibited practices;[3] (2) that a government agency be set up "to consider group practices brought before it." Its "opinions would be binding on enforcement agencies to prevent their using approved practices as the basis of investigation or prosecution." Where an "honest difference of opinion between an industry and the board" existed, the matter could be

---

[1] Resale price maintenance means an arrangement under which the supplier fixes the price at which his customer, the distributor, must sell the goods.

[2] Canadian Chamber of Commerce, Brief by the Executive Council, August 4, 1950, pp. 2, 3; Fowler, R. M., Memorandum to the Special Committee Studying the Combines Investigation Act, September 1950, pp. 7, 8; Canadian Retail Federation, Memorandum Submitted to the Committee to Study the Combines Investigation Act, September 15, 1950, p. 5 and *passim*.

[3] R. M. Fowler, Memorandum to the Special Committee, pp. 12, 13, 14.

settled by civil process initiated either by the industry or the combines commissioner in the form of a "cease and desist" application.[4]

Another objection raised in the business briefs was directed at the autonomy of the combines commissioner and especially at his power to have his report published irrespective of the attitude of the minister. The Canadian Chamber of Commerce brief made the following points: "The Commissioner should be responsible to the Minister, and in no case should his authority exceed that of the Minister .... No investigation should be undertaken by the Commissioner without the consent of the Minister .... No remission of a report, etc., should be made to a provincial Attorney-General without the consent of the Minister .... The Commissioner's report of a Combines Investigation should not be published before conviction."[5] Some business submissions opposed all publication and suggested that the commissioner report to the minister alone, who would decide "whether the evidence adduced constitutes an infringement of the Act."[6]

The opinion that the Commissioner and his staff were biased against business ran through the briefs. Mr. Fowler said: "There has been gross unfairness in publishing the reports of the Commissioner before prosecution. The inquiry has been conducted with such secrecy, with such a prejudiced approach, and with such a lack of full knowledge of the industry, that publication of the report has offended against the basic concept of fair trial in criminal cases. These reports are accepted by the public as accurate and complete, when they have often been neither."[7]

Complaints were registered against the methods employed by combines officers. These included: the "seizure and impounding of company records; the secrecy and non-disclosure of evidence taken during an inquiry; the failure to disclose the nature of

----

[4] *Ibid.*, pp. 15, 16.

[5] Submission of the Executive Council of the Canadian Chamber of Commerce to the Committee to Study the Combines Investigation Act, August 4, 1950, pp. 3, 4. See also Brief of the Canadian Electrical Manufacturers' Association, September 20, 1950, p. 2.

[6] Memorandum Submitted to the Committee to Study the Combines Investigation Act by the Canadian Retail Federation, September 15, 1950, p. 4.

[7] Fowler, Memorandum to the Special Committee, p. 21.

charges against an industry and the virtual refusal of an opportunity to make an explanation or reply; the preparation of one-sided and prejudiced reports; and the publication of such reports which do great damage to the public reputation of an industry which later has frequently been found guiltless by the courts."[8]

There were also objections to some of the methods of handling combines cases for prosecution. Some felt that access should be permitted to all the evidence in the possession of the commissioner.[9] Others condemned that section of the Combines Investigation Act which makes corporations *prima facie* responsible for statements in documents found in the possession of their employees. This, it was suggested, shifts the burden of proof from the Crown to the accused.[10] Some business briefs claimed the right of trial by judge *and jury* for corporations, since this right is granted to individuals and since the matter may involve deciding "what may, or may not, be detrimental to the public."[11] Others requested that the right of the Exchequer Court to suspend or cancel patents when used as a monopoly device be ended.[12]

The committee had specifically requested comments on resale price maintenance. Generally, business interests favoured this practice on the ground that it prevented or limited the use of the "loss-leader,"[13] or that it enabled the manufacturer to induce the retailer to service the product after it has been sold, or that it provided assurance to the manufacturer "that his goods will be distributed in an orderly manner."[14] Other reasons were also advanced, such as keeping prices down in periods of short supply,

[8] *Ibid.*, p. 20.

[9] Brief of the Canadian Electrical Manufacturers' Association, November 21, 1951, p. 2.

[10] Submission of the Executive Council of the Canadian Chamber of Commerce to the Committee to Study the Combines Investigation Act, August 4, 1950, p. 5.

[11] *Ibid.*

[12] *Ibid.*, p. 5 and appendix.

[13] Memorandum Submitted to the Committee to Study the Combines Investigation Act by the Canadian Retail Federation, September 15, 1950, p. 2 and appendix A. A "loss-leader" is an article sold below cost for the purpose of attracting business.

[14] Brief of the Canadian Electrical Manufacturers' Association, September 20, 1950, p. 4.

preventing "predatory price cutting,"[15] keeping prices uniform in large and small centres, maintaining the reputation of the article, and so on.

It is evident that most of the recommendations from the business community would have weakened the enforcement of the act by requiring that a specific detriment be proven, reducing the powers of the commissioner, permitting resale price maintenance, or altering the requirements and procedures of judicial enforcement. In contrast, the recommendations of the Canadian Federation of Agriculture and the Canadian Labour Congress were in favour of strong and effective anti-monopoly action.

The agricultural brief took the view that the farmer operates under "conditions of free competition" whereas many of the goods he must buy are "produced and sold under conditions of imperfect competition and semi-monopoly." "By restricting production, very often by definite arrangement, industrialists maintain their price structures and transfer productive workers to the unemployment roll."[16] The federation made three specific recommendations: (1) It opposed any amendments to the act which might "limit the powers of the Commissioner to initiate studies on his own, . . . place limitations upon the publishing of reports by the Combines Commissioner, . . . or give legal sanction to certain types of agreements to restrict production or eliminate price competition." (2) It favoured making resale price maintenance an illegal practice. (3) It recommended an amendment to the Criminal Code "to provide that conditional sales . . . should be declared an illegal practice."[17]

The Canadian Congress of Labour was, like the Canadian Federation of Agriculture, in favour of strengthening anti-combines action. It pointed out that a "trust-busting crusade" would not be practical and that public regulation of monopolistic corporations would be inefficient because it would involve "the maintenance of two managements, one private and one public,

[15] *Ibid.*

[16] Presentation of the Canadian Federation of Agriculture to the Special Committee Appointed by the Government of Canada for the Purpose of Studying the Combines Investigation Act, August 17, 1950, pp. 1, 2.

[17] *Ibid.*, pp. 8, 9. A conditional sale is one in which the buyer is required to purchase, in addition, another article or class of articles from the seller.

overlapping and interfering with each other." It stated its preference for outright public operation, but recognized that "the Canadian people have not voted for this policy, and that it is outside the Committee's terms of reference."[18]

Its recommendations involved putting "mergers, trusts or monopolies" on the same footing as "combines," and strengthening the requirements relating to the publication of reports to prevent delay by the minister.[19] The brief ended with a defence of the commissioner against a charge of bias brought by the General Manager of the Canadian Manufacturers' Association.

After hearing representations from all interested parties and pursuing its own studies, the MacQuarrie Committee issued its report in two parts. On October 1, 1951, it reported on the question of resale price maintenance, and its final report appeared on March 8, 1952. It found that resale price maintenance was "a real and undesirable restriction on competition by private agreement or 'law' and its general tendency is to discourage economic efficiency." It condemned the "loss-leader" but felt that it did not pose a serious problem in a period of inflation and relative scarcity. It recommended that it be made an offence for a manufacturer or other supplier to recommend, prescribe, or enforce minimum resale prices for his products.[20]

The final report of the committee related to four areas: administration, prohibited practices, remedies for infractions, and research. The administrative recommendations reflected agreement with the criticisms of the business community that the commissioner was both a prosecutor and judge. The committee recommended that these functions be divided between an investigation and research agency, which should retain the initiative in investigation, and a board, which should hear the submissions of the agency and the "accused" parties and report its findings. The committee opposed the narrowing of the range of prohibited practices that would have resulted from a requirement that

[18] Submission of the Canadian Congress of Labour to the Committee to Study the Combines Investigation Act, August 1950, p. 2.

[19] *Ibid.*, pp. 3, 4.

[20] *Report of the Committee to Study Combines Legislation* (Ottawa, 1952), p. 71; hereafter cited as MacQuarrie *Report.*

"specific detriment" be proven. With regard to remedies, the committee favoured consolidating the anti-combines sections of the Criminal Code with the Combines Investigation Act. It reported against trial by jury for corporations and against a statutory limit on fines in combines cases. It favoured restraining orders to stop combines from continuing illegal practices, and it urged that offenders be obliged to report to the court after conviction to show that the combine was not being continued. It also supported the use of tariff, patent, and other remedial action instead of relying solely on the criminal law. It recommended close liaison between the board and other departments whose activities may affect monopolistic situations and practices.

A major recommendation concerned research. It is clear from the committee's report that this was regarded as one of supreme importance. The committee proposed that research should be the task of a special division of the investigation and research agency and continued:

Research in the field of monopolistic situations and practices should become one of the most important assignments of the investigation and research agency. Information concerning this aspect of the organization and the working of our economy is badly lacking in Canada. Very few studies have been made in this field and they are all incomplete and often out-dated.

Such a situation can easily be explained. The job to be done is so complex and wide in scope that it cannot be carried on an individual basis without any integrated and long-range plan. Furthermore, private individuals and research organizations cannot be expected to fulfil that function adequately because, apart from financial limitations, they are not in a position to get the necessary information. In this field more than in any other, businessmen are reluctant to answer questions, to give the facts and disclose their secrets. On the other hand, in government, the only agency that could have been interested in this type of research was the Combines Investigation Commission. However, research up to now has been only a secondary task, and usually its relatively small staff was completely absorbed in the actual work of investigations. It is not surprising, then, that so little is known about monopolistic situations and practices in Canada.

A sound programme of empirical research on this vast subject is much needed at present. At least our main industries should be the objects of continuing study and observations. Facts should be systematically assembled concerning the behaviour of an industry and its current policies bearing on prices, production, innovation, investment, costs, profits, market areas, business practices, the use of patents, corporate structures and inter-relations as well as any other matter affecting competitive conditions. We need to know much more in detail than we now do about the various aspects of the movement of concentration of economic power in Canada. Large business units raise a special problem for public policy but factual knowledge is much too scanty to warrant any specific proposal. Judgment on the giant enterprise cannot be final before extensive empirical research has provided the facts concerning their organization, their processes of business policy formation and their performance. Our knowledge in the wide field of monopolistic practices is just as inadequate. Such practices as discrimination, "loss-leaders," price leadership, tying contracts, combination sales, advertising, basing-point systems and probably many others should be subjected to empirical studies in order to know their extent, their operation, their effects, and the remedies to cope with them, if necessary. Finally some attention should be given to the field of remedies in order to add to the rather restricted list of weapons we are now using to combat undesirable monopolistic situations and practices.

A research programme defined along these general lines would serve several important purposes. First, it would afford great assistance to investigators in indicating the dangerous spots in our economy that need to be closely watched and in supplying up-to-date and pertinent preliminary information. Thus, investigations could be more carefully planned, the sectors to be investigated could be selected after consideration of the overall picture and the points to be covered by investigations could be precisely defined. Second, in some cases, factual studies would make the ordinary investigation unnecessary and would permit a more rapid application of the law. Third, it would put the emphasis on the most desirable remedy in each case, thus in many instances, where the possibilities of restoring competition are remote, supplying means of correction superior to criminal prosecution. Gradually, it would be possible to get an adequate idea of the sector of our economy which is competitive and which should remain so; a better knowledge would also be provided of the composition and working of the other sector which is likely to remain monopolistic. Fourth, the publication of such research studies would greatly contribute to inform the public about the performance of our economy and to avoid the spreading of prejudices caused by ignorance.

If exploitation and unfairness exist, the public has the right to know it; on the other hand, if private enterprise is efficient and alert, it has the right to be protected against prejudices and unjust demands. Finally, factual studies and the constant search for new remedies will enable Parliament to improve our anti-monopoly legislation and to adapt it to the changing requirements of the public interest.[21]

21 *Ibid.*, pp. 43-4.

4. The Revised Legislation

Parliament considered the preliminary report of the Mac-Quarrie Committee relating to resale price maintenance in December 1951. The government brought down a bill incorporating the committee's recommendations to outlaw this practice, and a heated debate ensued. The Conservative opposition tried to prevent passage on the grounds that no provisions against "loss-leader" selling were included, and that insufficient opportunities had been made available for hearing witnesses and studying the probable effects of the legislation. The C.C.F., which would have preferred a public authority to control prices, voted with the government. The amendment was passed and made it an offence to fix minimum resale prices, although suggested resale prices were still permitted.

In May 1952, the government presented a bill to Parliament incorporating many of the other reconmmendations made by the MacQuarrie Committee. From the outset of the debate, substantially unanimous support met the bill, and it passed third reading without debate.

The new legislation divided the functions of the commissioner between two new bodies: the Director of Investigation and Research and the Restrictive Trade Practices Commission. The director was to have a staff of investigators to look into complaints. He could conduct investigations on his own initiative and discontinue an inquiry on his own authority unless it had reached the point where he had submitted evidence before the Commission.[1] He must, however, report the discontinuance of a formal investigation to the minister, showing the information obtained and the reason for discontinuing the investigation. The powers of inquiry were extended to cover "monopolistic situations" even where no breach of the statute was suspected.

The Commission was to consist of not more than three persons, who were to hold office during good behaviour for ten years and be eligible for reappointment. It was to consider the evidence of the director and hear the "defence" of the parties investigated. It was then to write a report to the minister, reviewing the evidence, appraising the effect on the public interest of the arrangements revealed, and recommending remedies. The minister was to publish this report within thirty days, unless the Commission should advise against publication, in which case he could make his own decision.

One change was made in the definition of prohibited practices. Section 498 A of the Criminal Code was amended so as not to prohibit an isolated act of price discrimination, but only the systematic practice of it. This change was not of great practical importance since there has not been a prosecution for price discrimination either before or since the amendment.

Remedies somewhat stronger than previously were provided in cases where convictions had been obtained. The courts were empowered to issue orders for the discontinuance or against the repetition of an offence. This included the power to require the dissolution of a merger or monopoly. Convicted firms could be required to furnish continuing reports on their activities. The ceiling on fines was removed.

In comparing the new legislation with the proposals of the various groups that have been surveyed, it may be seen that the

---

[1] 1 Elizabeth II, c. 39, s. 14(1), An Act to Amend the Combines Investigation Act and the Criminal Code.

revision ended the concentration of powers in the hands of a single individual, to which both the government and business interests had been opposed. The director could still initiate inquiries, but the powers needed to pursue an inquiry effectively, by examining witnesses, seizing documents, and ordering written returns, could be exercised only after authorization by a member of the three-man Commission. More important still was the transfer to the new Commission of the power to decide that a public report should be made, as well as the writing of the report itself. The minister was still required to publish the report (within thirty days), but a public report "accusing" a firm or group of firms now in effect required the concurrence of several persons, the director and the commissioners, instead of the decision of one.

On the other hand, the new legislation implemented none of the proposals for the weakening of the substantive provisions of the Combines Investigation Act, which had been repeatedly advanced by business interests and had, as indicated by Mr. McGregor's memorandum, been considered by at least some members of the Cabinet. On the contrary, the only significant change in the definition of offences added resale price maintenance to the list. Moreover, the machinery for legal enforcement was strengthened by the various provisions listed above.

Most of the suggestions of the MacQuarrie Committee were carried out, but there were some striking exceptions. The very important recommendation relating to research was not implemented. Instead of setting up a separate division with its own director to carry out a research programme, the amendment combined the two functions of "investigation" and "research" under one director, whose experience and training were mainly legal.[2] The result has been to place the emphasis on "investigation," which yields concrete results in terms of evidence leading to prosecution. More general research has been neglected.

[2] Mr. T. D. MacDonald had been the Deputy Attorney-General of Nova Scotia from 1940 to 1949, when he became Superintendent of Bankruptcy for the federal Department of Justice. In 1950 he became Commissioner, Combines Investigation Act, and, with the amendment of that act in 1952, he was named the new Director of Investigation and Research.

Other recommendations of the MacQuarrie Committee that were not implemented concerned the use of federal government powers in various fields to back up an anti-monopoly policy. There were already clauses in the Combines Investigation Act authorizing the use of the power over tariffs and patents where a combine had been found, and the committee made recommendations for broadening the authority and putting it to practical use. More generally, it suggested that in each case "the various aspects of the federal government's policy should be carefully reviewed ... to see if they could be used as effective remedies," and that to this end "administrative arrangements should be established so as to ensure close liaison and permanent contact between the Board and other departments of government."[3] Practically none of this was put into effect.

It is evident that the legislation of 1952 was a compromise involving something for everybody and satisfaction for none. Stronger enforcement provision and prohibition of resale price maintenance reflected the influence of the former Commissioner, the MacQuarrie Committee, and all those, in Parliament and public life, who regarded monopoly as a serious menace to the economy. The separation of functions, while also following the recommendation of the committee, reflected the interests of those, in business and in the government, who wished to minimize the interference with business arrangements. Also it met the lawyer's objection to one person acting as "prosecutor and judge." The failure to implement the recommendations for research and for the use of federal powers outside the criminal law also tended to minimize the effectiveness of anti-combines action.

One can, however, detect elements of a consistent policy behind the appearance of *ad hoc* compromise. There were, and are, two fundamentally different conceptions of the role of anti-trust legislation in the modern economy. According to one view, the major function of the anti-combines machinery is to prepare the prosecution and punishment of a small minority among businessmen who abuse positions of economic power or engage in unfair practices. These men are criminals, and the criminal

---

[3] MacQuarrie *Report,* p. 49.

law is the basic tool for dealing with them. Evidently influential business groups hold this view of the role of the combines legislation, with its corollary that it is "unfair" to use the investigative machinery on businessmen engaging in "normal" trade practices, who are stigmatized as criminals when it becomes known that the "combines cops" are investigating them.

The alternative view holds that the propensity to monopolize, being part and parcel of the propensity to seek maximum profit, is common to all businessmen and not the special characteristic of a criminal minority. This is the meaning of Adam Smith's much-quoted statement that "people of the same trade seldom meet together ... but the conversation ends in conspiracy against the public or in some contrivance to raise prices." In the ideal economy analysed by Adam Smith and his successors, this tendency was held in check by the existence of a large number of competing firms in each line of business and by ease of entry for new competitors. In the modern economy, in which many lines of business are highly concentrated in a small number of firms, and the entry of new competitors on an economical scale is often difficult, the effectiveness of the checks on monopoly is much reduced. The preservation of competition therefore requires constant attention by the government in order to render the economic environment competitive and to reduce the attractiveness of monopolistic arrangements. In shaping the economic environment all the government's economic powers and activities are relevant, and the enforcement of specific anti-monopoly rules and regulations is only a part, and not necessarily the most important part, of an anti-monopoly policy. Moreover, this view implies that businessmen may find themselves in monopolistic situations simply by pursuing "sensible" business policies, so that, on the one hand, their investigation by the combines machinery does not signify that they are regarded as "criminals," and on the other hand the fact that the businessman's behaviour is normal offers no reason why his arrangements should not be interfered with in the interest of competition.

On the hypothesis that the government followed the first view rather than the second, all aspects of the 1952 legislation can be seen to fit into a consistent pattern. If legal proceedings against a criminal minority are the objective, the strengthening of the legal enforcement machinery makes sense. Moreover, given this objective, the application of the legal analogy to the administrative arm is relevant, and the claim that the role of judge and prosecutor should not be combined has weight. Further, in this view research is clearly of minor importance, its legitimate scope being confined to detective work or, at the most, work directly applicable to the question of modifying the legal rules and regulations. Finally, there is little need for liaison with other government departments. The application of remedies through the tariff, patents, and so forth, must wait on a finding of guilt, in which case such remedies at best supplement the fines or prison sentences provided by law.

A good case can be made for the theory that this view of the Combines Act was historically "legitimate" in the sense that it was held by Mackenzie King, the "father" of our anti-combines legislation, and also, at least before the war, by Mr. McGregor, the Commissioner.[4] It was not, however, the view held by the MacQuarrie Committee. This is evident in the great stress placed by the committee on the need for research and on the need to evaluate government activity in every economic field from the point of view of its impact on the monopoly problem. The committee's adherence to the alternative view also emerged in statements such as the following: "The monopoly problem takes many forms, it is highly complex, and requires continuous and careful examination.... Private monopolistic control, which cannot be completely eliminated, must be restrained and subjected to public review. The measures taken must be adaptable to complex and rapidly changing problems."[5] "Electorates and legislatures ... must be both alert and resourceful in discouraging the spread of monopoly."[6]

In the 1952 revision of the combines legislation, therefore, the

[4] On any other view it would be difficult to explain why the scope of combines activity before the war was so very limited, although McGregor apparently felt that (except during the Conservative regime) he was getting all the funds and staff that he needed. See *Hansard*, 1946, p. 3088.

[5] MacQuarrie *Report*, p. 27.

[6] *Ibid.*, p. 22.

government adhered to the narrower view of the functions of the Combines Act that was sanctioned by history and favoured by business. It rejected the broader conception implicit in the proposals of the MacQuarrie Committee.

5. The Machinery

WITH THE ENACTMENT of the amendment to the Combines Investigation Act, the Commissioner, Mr. T. D. MacDonald, was named Director of Investigation and Research. He retained control of the investigative and research staff and continued to report to the minister of justice. A Restrictive Trade Practices Commission was named, consisting of Mr. C. Rhodes Smith as Chairman and Messrs. Guy Favreau and A. S. Whiteley as members. It proceeded to hear the evidence of the director and the "defence" of the "accused" parties, and it wrote reports based on this information to the minister.

The revised legislation empowered the director to commence investigations of industries where an offence is suspected or to initiate broad inquiries into "monopolistic situations." All but three of the cases reported on have been of the former sort.

The procedure adopted for them is as follows. The director commences an investigation when: (1) he receives an official complaint lodged by six citizens; (2) he is instructed to do so by the minister of justice; or (3) he decides to do so on his own initiative. In practice, inquiries are mainly the result of informal complaints or newspaper reports. From fiscal year 1951/2 to 1958/9, the branch looked into 815 complaints and made 31 formal reports to the minister. Yet there were only three formal complaints from six citizens and no cases of formal direction by the minister.[1]

The decision as to how far to carry an inquiry is largely the director's. The permission of the Restrictive Trade Practices Commission is required for dropping a case only after the inquiry has reached the point where evidence has been brought before the Commission. The act states that when a case is dropped, the director must report in writing to the minister, showing the information obtained and the reasons for discontinuance, "but it does not indicate when a matter is to be considered as reaching a stage of formality such that its discontinuance must be reported under this section. It is the practice to report, under section 14, the discontinuance of any inquiry in which any power ... of compulsorily obtaining evidence, was exercised," and also certain other inquiries that "have involved considerable informal seeking of information. Below this level, however, a large number of complaints are considered each year and not pursued because it becomes apparent ... that the complaint is not warranted or that evidence relating to it cannot be obtained."[2] Unlike the American practice there is no requirement that all cases be disposed of by a written ruling,[3] and as a result great discretion is left in the hands of the director and the minister.

The preliminary investigation is conducted by a combines investigation officer, and consists of the collection of the "street information" or the generally available facts about the industry. These are found in the press (particularly the financial papers and trade journals), the publications of the Dominion Bureau of Statistics and other government agencies, and other public sources. On the basis of this preliminary investigation, the director decides whether the case is to be carried further.

---

[1] *Report of the Director of Investigation and Research, Combines Investigation Act, 1959,* p. 38; hereafter cited as *Annual Report.*

[2] *Ibid.,* p. 26.

[3] Federal Trade Commission, Rules of Practice and Procedure, May 1955, pp. 25-6.

The description of cases that were "dropped" at an early stage, contained in the annual reports of the director, suggests that there is a tendency to keep down the amount of investigation and research that is undertaken. In cases where the preliminary investigation of a complaint yields results that are conflicting or inconclusive, the Combines Branch often drops the investigation. For example, on a complaint from a dealer, charging price discrimination by a manufacturer of television sets, "information was obtained by interview from the complaining dealer and by interview and informal questionnaire from the manufacturer. Because the information so obtained was inconclusive and conflicting, it was considered that a more formal investigation was not warranted and the complainant was so advised."[4] A more vigorous policy would have resulted in a broadened investigation of the sales practices of television manufacturers.

If the director decides that a matter should be carried further, the documents to support a case are collected. Since this usually involves a visit to the premises of the firms involved, this action is taken only when the director is reasonably confident that the law is being broken in a significant way. An order is secured which has been signed by the director and a member of the Commission. Using this as authority, a team under the direction of a combines investigation officer visits the premises and searches the company's records for evidence. All documents which appear to be germane to the matter under investigation are seized. Each document is numbered and coded to indicate where it was obtained and to prevent loss. The documents are taken to Ottawa for copying and must be returned to the owner within forty days.[5]

This search procedure is the stage in the investigation which is objected to most strongly by businessmen and lawyers. They see it as an invasion of privacy, a disruption of their business affairs, and a singling out of businessmen for treatment appropriate to common criminals. Since the search authority is issued by the Commission and not a judge, some businessmen feel that

4 *Annual Report*, 1958, pp. 28-9.

5 1 Eliz. II, c. 39, ss. 9, 10, An Act to Amend the Combines Investigation Act and the Criminal Code.

they are denied legal and impartial consideration of the justification for the search. Moreover, since the practices of the Federal Trade Commission in the United States do not provide for searches of business premises without warning, Canadian businessmen often feel that the search procedure employed under the Combines Investigation Act is unwarrantably severe.[6] However, it offers the only means of obtaining certain types of evidence.

After the documents have been copied and studied, the next step is the taking of sworn testimony from the officials of the organizations under investigation. This will be taken before a hearings officer who to date has always been one of the members of the Commission. The evidence is taken down by a court stenographer. The testimony of one company is usually taken without persons from other firms being present. If no objection is raised, such persons may, however, be present, if it is thought the investigation would be furthered by their attendance. Witnesses are free to present evidence beyond that asked by the director, either by statement or by filing documents.

The director or the combines officer designated by him, on the basis of the information collected thus far, then normally requires the parties under investigation to submit written returns under oath, in answer to specific questions posed.

Thus there are normally four stages in the director's investigation: (1) the collection of "street" information; (2) the collection of documents; (3) the taking of the oral transcript of evidence; (4) the taking of written returns under oath.

In some cases all four stages are not employed, and the sequence is not necessarily as indicated. Naturally, at any point the director may discontinue the investigation, and, unless stage 3 has been reached, he may discontinue it without reference to the Commission. If he decides to carry the case further, he has a "Statement of Evidence" prepared. This is often a voluminous document, mimeographed on legal-size paper and containing a description and analysis of the industry along with the director's

---

[6] In the United States, the Federal Trade Commission "may issue a notice to grant access to, for examination and copying, documentary evidence of any corporation being investigated." Federal Trade Commission, Rules of Practice and Procedure, May 1955, p. 8.

allegations and detailed supporting evidence. It is not a public document, but is made available to the parties "accused" and to the Commission. It comprises the substance of the director's case which the parties named must answer, although the director is free to withhold some evidence from the statement and to introduce it later in the hearing before the Commission.

The proceedings before the Commission are held in private to avoid prejudicing the interests of the accused by a piecemeal and partial divulging of evidence against them. The director is usually represented by the combines officer who has directed the investigation to date. He may have legal training, or he may be an economics or commerce graduate. The firms under investigation are represented by their lawyers. The proceedings begin with the submission of evidence by both sides. Since the director's findings are contained in his summary of evidence, the accused parties are aware of the allegations they face and have an adequate opportunity of meeting them. On the other hand the director or his representative may not be aware of the case the "accused" proposes to make. Sometimes the Commission receives an outline of the "defence" in advance of the hearing, which is made available to the director. This is, however, not required. In any case it is only a sketchy outline and does not really forewarn the director and his representative. Thus the "accused" parties have an advantage analogous to that enjoyed by the defendant in a criminal trial. After the evidence is in, the director or his representative states his conclusions on the evidence, counsel for each of the accused replies, and the director may then make a brief rebuttal. Sometimes supplementary briefs or statements are filed after the proceedings to clear up questions of fact.

Expert witnesses such as economists or accountants may appear for either side before the Commission. The Commision itself can also call such witnesses to "appraise the arrangements and practices," or employ its own consultants for this purpose.

The proceedings before the Commission then involve both legal arguments relating to the alleged infractions of the anti-combines legislation, and also economic argument, concerned mainly with the structure of the industry and the effect of the monopolistic arrangements. In the conspiracy cases (the majority of cases) the legal arguments predominate, but in merger, and presumably in monopoly cases as well, more emphasis would be placed on economic factors.

After the hearings the Commission writes its report to the minister. This is a lengthy document, presenting a description and analysis of the industry and outlining the events that have led its members to be accused of contraventions of the law. While the report is required to "contain recommendations as to the application of remedies,"[7] it does not normally make a specific recommendation regarding prosecution.

The Commission has been handicapped by the fact that from 1957/8 to 1960 there were only two commissioners. The rate at which reports can be completed is restricted by the fact that the commissioners, separately or jointly, must hear verbal evidence on each case, both before and after the presentation of the Statement of Evidence, must study the documents in each case, and must personally write the reports. Until recently the Commission's permanent staff consisted only of clerical personnel, but in 1959 an economist was added. In some cases the Commission has retained an economist as consultant.

One of the most controversial aspects of the Canadian anti-combines policy is the requirement that the Commission's reports be published.[8] Business interests have criticized the publication of the reports before an adverse judicial decision has been handed down, on the grounds that the firms are being injured before they have been found guilty of any offence. On the other hand, proponents of the policy have pointed out that the reports are factual accounts of situations and arrangements existing in industry of which the public has a right to be apprised. Also, they argue, the likelihood of being caught out and having their activities publicly known is the greatest incentive to businessmen to conduct their affairs not only within the letter but also within the spirit of the law. These points of view each have their spokesman within both of the leading political parties.

The reports have always been detailed and factual. They have

<hr>

[7] Combines Investigation Act, Office Consolidation 1952, s. 19(1).

[8] See pp. 27-8.

been written for the serious student and not for the general reader who would find them dry as dust. They do, however, contain material that journalists might use in a popular form. The format of the reports has always been austere. The plain yellow cover and closely printed reports of the pre-1952 commissioner were perhaps typical of the "pre-public relations era" government report. The grey-covered reports of the Restrictive Trade Practices Commission, reproduced by an offset process from copy done on an electric typewriter, are a drab contrast to eye-catching material currently being issued by other departments of government. Their length, dullness, and drab format have served to make them one of the most uninviting of all government publications.

Recently, two thousand copies of the Commission's report were printed. There is a general mailing list of about eight hundred names, including university and general reference libraries, trade associations, interested public officials, research workers, and members of the general public. A somewhat larger list receives the annual report of the Director of Investigation and Research, which constitutes a more attractive, although still austere, publication. Copies of all reports are made available to the members of both houses of Parliament.

When the Commission's report is made public, the director issues a press release informing the Parliamentary Press Gallery, the Canadian Press, and the British United Press of the report. Until 1957, this release was a balanced summary of the report, drawn up by the combines officer who directed the investigation. It was submitted to the director, the Commission, and the minister for review and approval before being issued to the press. No public relations officer was involved at any stage. Since 1957 the press release has not involved a summary of the report at all. It has simply consisted of an announcement that the report has been published. The journalists have been left to peruse the report itself for their stories. Under such conditions extensive press coverage is unlikely as editors and reporters are busy men, accustomed to receiving their government information in a more finished form. As a result the reports have passed with very little notice in the press.

With the issuing of the report the Commission's responsibilities are discharged. The decision whether to prosecute or not must be made by the minister of justice personally. As a result it is essentially a political or policy decision. Indeed the matter could be of such moment as to involve the Cabinet. This is, in fact, necessary if action other than prosecution is contemplated, such as a change in the tariff. If the minister favours prosecution he sends the evidence to an outside lawyer for his opinion. If the lawyer recommends prosecution, he will normally be retained to conduct the case in the courts. Following the Canadian convention, the lawyer selected is a supporter of the party in power. In the Canadian Breweries case, a Liberal lawyer was replaced by a Conservative after the change of government in 1957.

Usually the office of the Director of Investigation and Research provides advice and assistance in the preparation of the prosecution's case. The lawyer in charge, however, plans the prosecution's strategy and selects the evidence to be presented. The tendency has been to emphasize legal argument and to avoid economic analysis. Naturally, busy senior counsel are not inclined to introduce complex economic arguments with which they are not fully familiar, and to which they do not expect criminal court judges to be receptive.

There is no requirement that an investigation be completed within any stated period. While some investigations are completed in a short time, others may take up to eight years before reaching the courts.[9] When an investigation takes place over a protracted period, the firms concerned are likely to abandon the offending practice long before the question of prosecution is considered. In such a case it is possible that no legal action will be taken. In other words, the investigation itself may have remedial effects.[10]

---

[9] The investigation of the brewing industry was begun in 1951 (*Annual Report*, 1956, p. 9) and came before the courts in 1959.

[10] The resale price maintenance of bread in a small city in southern Ontario is a case in point. The 1953 *Annual Report* states: "If in fact there has been present any disregard for the provisions of section 34 of the Act, . . . it would appear that the inquiries made had brought home to the parties concerned the irregularity of their conduct and led them to correct it" (pp. 24-5). The case was dropped.

Price fixing by dump truck operators supplying sand and gravel is another such

TABLE I

TIME PERIOD FOR DISPOSING OF CASES NOT LEADING TO PROSECUTION
1956, 1957, and 1958*

Case	Opening date	Discontinuance date	Time period (months)
Merger of pulp and paper companies	May/56 (S)	July/57	15
Molasses	Mar./56 (S)	Aug./57	17
Anaesthetic gases	Oct./57 (C & I)	Aug./58	10
Storage batteries	Mar./57 (Q)	Aug./58	17
Sand and gravel	July/57 (Q)	Oct./57	3
Confectionery	July/56 (S)	July/57	12
TV sets: price discrimination	Mar./57 (Q)	May/57	1
Coffee	Aug./57 (Q)	Sept./57	1
Electrical equipment	June/54 (S)	Mar./56	21
Building materials	Not available		
Firearms	July/56 (S)	Feb./57	7
Motion picture films	July/56 (I)	Oct./56	3
C.N.R. & Hilton	June/55 (H)	Dec./55	6

S: Search authority issued.

C: Correspondence commenced.

I: First interviews commenced.

Q: First questionnaire sent out.

H: Question in the House of Commons.

* The cases listed are those discussed in the Director's *Annual Report* for the years ended March 31, 1956, 1957, and 1958, under the heading "Other Cases."

---

case. The 1958 *Annual Report* stated: "The solicitors [for the accused parties] ... advised that any arrangement entered into had been discontinued. In view of this information, the inquiry was discontinued subject to be reopened should information of additional activities of the same character on the part of the members of the association come to light." (Pp. 26-7.)

TABLE II

TIME PERIOD BETWEEN FIRST SEARCH AUTHORITY AND COMMISSION'S REPORT
Cases in Court, 1956, 1957, and 1958*

Case	Date of first search authority	Date of report	Time period (months)
Fine papers	Nov./48	Oct./52	47
Electrical wire and cable	Nov./50	Nov./53	36
Wire fencing	Aug./52	Nov./54	26
Beer	July/51	May/55	46
Asphalt roofing	June/52	Aug./55	38
Transmission and Conveyor equipment	Mar./53	Dec./55	33
Winnipeg coal	Jan./53	Jan./56	36
Quilting	Apr./54	Mar./56	23
Boxboard	May/54	June/56	25
Western sugar	Aug./55	Jan./57	16
Coarse papers	Nov./48	Jan./53	50
Vancouver gasoline	July/51	Feb./54	31
Household appliances	June/54	Oct./55	16
Rubber	Sept./47	May/52	56
Timmins coal	July/53	Nov./54	16

* The cases listed are those discussed in the Director's *Annual Report* for the years ended March 31, 1956, 1957, and 1958, under the headings "Proceedings Arising out of Previous Reports" and "Cases in Court."

Generally cases that are dropped are disposed of in a shorter period than those that ultimately go before the courts. This is shown in Tables I and II, relating to cases in the annual reports of the director for 1956, 1957, and 1958. The date for the opening of the cases is either the date when the first search authority was issued, or, if there was none, the date of the first questionnaire, correspondence, interview, or question in the House.[11]

To date there have been only three reports on general inquiries

[11] The dates were supplied by the Director on request.

into monopolistic situations. They deal with loss-leader selling, discriminatory pricing practices in the grocery trade, and rate fixing in automobile insurance. In such an investigation, material is collected by the director's staff through questionnaires sent to parties in the affected trade, and through other means, and assembled into a volume which is printed and circulated for opinion and comment among those supplying information. In addition, trade associations and other interested parties receive copies, so that about eight hundred are distributed in all. These people are asked whether they wish public hearings permitting them to take issue with the report. If the answer is affirmative, hearings are held. In the case of the loss-leader investigation, four thousand pages of evidence were obtained in public hearings from twenty-nine organizations and twenty-four individual companies or persons.[12] In addition, the Commission invited two academic economists from the United States to appear at the hearings.

In the investigation of automobile insurance, the Commission held hearings for four days and also received briefs from interested parties. In both these cases the Commission wrote its own report, based on an evaluation of the material collected by the director, as well as on briefs and evidence obtained at the hearings. In the study on price discrimination in the grocery trade, the Commission simply reproduced the factual report of the director without evaluating the material or drawing conclusions. The explanation offered for this procedure was that no objection was raised to the material by the parties consulted.

[12] *Report of an Inquiry into Loss-Leader Selling* (Ottawa, 1955), p. 5.

6. Combines Administration Expenditures

IN THE FISCAL year 1959/60, expenditures under the Combines Investigation Act totalled half a million dollars,[1] while total federal government expenditures amounted to $5,700 million. It is evident that in terms of the expenditure involved, anti-combines activity is an insignificant part of over-all government operations.

The relative importance assigned to anti-combines activity can also be gauged by comparing the half-million dollar expenditure on this item with expenditures on other government operations. Some selected expenditures, for the same fiscal year, in millions of dollars are as follows: Canadian Government Travel Bureau, 2.3; Research in Agricultural Economics, 0.7; Newfoundland Bait Service, 0.5; Department of Labour Economics and Research Branch, 0.7; Governor General and Lieutenant-Governors, 0.4; Dominion Observatory: Administration, Operation, and Maintenance, 0.9; Administration of the Immigration Act (*excluding* Field and Inspectional Services), 1.2; Defence Research and Development, 39.2.

It is evident that, if more anti-combines activity were con-

---

[1] All figures on expenditure in this chapter are from the *Public Accounts of Canada*.

sidered necessary, expenditures could be increased four or five times without a significant impact on the government's finances.

There can also be no doubt that combines administration expenditures are small in comparison with the amounts large companies can spend in fighting combines cases, without a significant impact on their financial position. For example, a single company involved in a number of recent investigations, the Abitibi Power & Paper Company, had in 1959 net sales of $134 million and net profits before taxes of $25 million.

The staff of the two sections of the combines branch numbered fifty employees at the end of fiscal year 1958/9. Nineteen of these were in the professional grades (including the Director of Investigation and Research and the two members of the Restrictive Trade Practices Commission).[2] These figures do not, of course, include lawyers in private practice retained for opinions and prosecutions, and other expert consultants.

The changing volume of combines investigation activity, as measured by the annual expenditure under the Combines Investigation Act, is shown in Tables III, IV, and V and Charts I to IV. In Table III, actual expenditures are shown as well as expenditures in "real" terms, that is, in dollars of constant (1949) purchasing power. The next two columns show combines expenditures as a proportion of the Gross National Product. As a rough first approximation, it may be said that the potential need for anti-combines activity varies in proportion to the volume of economic activity, so that these columns are a rough measure of changes in the amount of anti-combines activity in relation to the need for it. Finally, the table and charts show combines investigation expenditures as a proportion of total federal government non-military expenditures on goods and services, as an indication of the relative importance assigned to anti-combines activity in relation to other federal government civilian activity.

Since fiscal year 1953/4 the Public Accounts show expenditures under the Combines Investigation Act separately for each of the two branches that were set up under the new legislation: the Director of Investigation and Research, and the Restrictive Trade

---

[2] Data from *Annual Report*, 1959.

TABLE III
COMBINES INVESTIGATION EXPENDITURE [1]

Fiscal year [2]	Expenditure A $000	Expenditure B $000	Expenditure in 1949 dollars [3] A $000	Expenditure in 1949 dollars [3] B $000	Expenditure per $ million of Gross National Product [4] A $	Expenditure per $ million of Gross National Product [4] B $	Expenditure per $ million of federal non-military expenditures on goods and services [4] A $	Expenditure per $ million of federal non-military expenditures on goods and services [4] B $
1936	3.4		5.7		0.79		26	
1937								
1938	14.6		23.2		2.79		124	
1939	52.5		82.4		9.94		375	
1940	45.3		71.6		8.03		316	
1941	61.8		94.0		9.16		451	
1942	57.5		82.6		6.90		408	
1943	23.4		32.1		2.27		173	
1944	25.2		34.0		2.27		165	
1945	24.9		33.4		2.10		146	
1946	34.6		46.1		2.92		168	
1947	77.6		100.1		6.55		337	
1948	124.8		147.2		9.48		311	
1949	169.4		174.6		11.20		388	
1950	168.8		168.8		10.33		332	
1951	221.1		214.9		12.28		457	
1952	205.8		181.0		9.72		378	
1953	267.0		229.1		11.13		387	
1954	393.7	329.2	340.8	285.0	15.73	13.16	604	505
1955	407.5	328.1	350.7	282.4	16.38	13.19	564	454
1956	426.5	361.5	366.4	310.6	15.72	13.32	569	482
1957	427.9	360.3	362.3	305.1	13.99	11.78	486	409
1958	372.9	319.9	306.0	262.4	11.74	10.07	388	333
1959	394.2	340.6	315.1	272.2	12.13	10.48	332	287
1960	541.9	475.4	428.4	375.0	15.67	13.75	431	379

[1] Expenditures under the Combines Investigation Act as shown in the *Public Accounts*.

[2] Twelve months ending March 31 of year shown.

[3] Expenditures divided by Consumer Price Index (1949 = 100) for calendar year preceding year shown.

[4] G.N.P. and federal expenditures on goods and services for calendar year preceding year shown.

A: Total Expenditure.

B: Expenditure for the Director of Investigation and Research (from 1954).

Sources: *Public Accounts, D.B.S. Prices and Price Indexes, D.B.S. National Accounts,* 1926-56, 1959, Tables 1, 37, 43 in each.

CHART I

COMBINES ADMINISTRATION EXPENDITURE

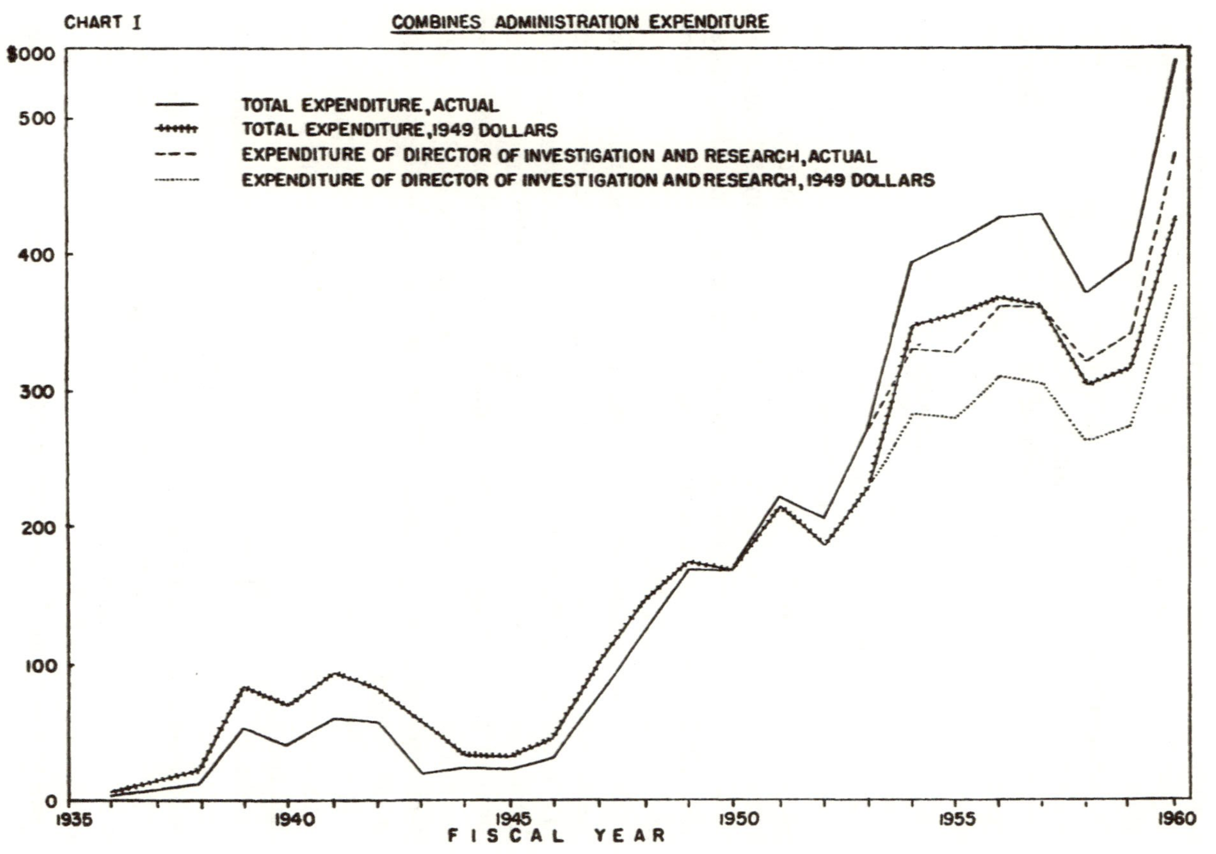

Practices Commission. Since, compared with the earlier anti-combines organization, the new arrangement involves a certain duplication of functions, total expenditure gives an exaggerated impression of the increase in activity. On the other hand, since the existence of the Commission relieves the director of certain activities previously the responsibility of the single commissioner and his staff, the expenditures of the director are too low in relation to earlier expenditures under the act to indicate the true trend of activity. The table and charts therefore show both total expenditures and those of the director, to indicate the upper and lower limits to the trend of activity.

Pre-war combines expenditures under Mr. McGregor rose from very low levels in the mid-thirties to a peak of nearly $100,000 (at 1949 prices) at the beginning of the war. Thereafter they were sharply curtailed as a result of the government decision to suspend anti-combines activity during the war. After fiscal year 1945/6, expenditures rose sharply, as a new series of major investigations was launched.

Mr. McGregor resigned at the end of 1949, but the completion of the investigations and cases he had launched drove expenditures to a peak of over $200,000 (at 1949 prices) in fiscal year 1950/1. After a drop in 1952, expenditures rose again, with the establishment of the new administrative machinery. Total expenditures reached a new peak of $366,000 (at 1949 prices) in 1956 and then declined, but shot up to $428,000 (at 1949 prices) in the last year of our period.

It is clear that the post-war level of activity under the Combines Investigation Act was far higher than the pre-war peak and that the level of activity since 1952 exceeded that under the old machinery. These facts are also reflected in the number of reports published. From 1930 to 1934, only four reports were published under the Combines Investigation Act, and between 1935 and 1939 only three. No reports were issued during the war, but in the three years 1947-9 six reports were published.[3] In the two years following Mr. McGregor's resignation no reports were put out, but in the next eight years, 1952-9, under the new

---

[3] In addition to the *Report on International Cartels,* published in 1945. .

CHART II

COMBINES ADMINISTRATION EXPENDITURE

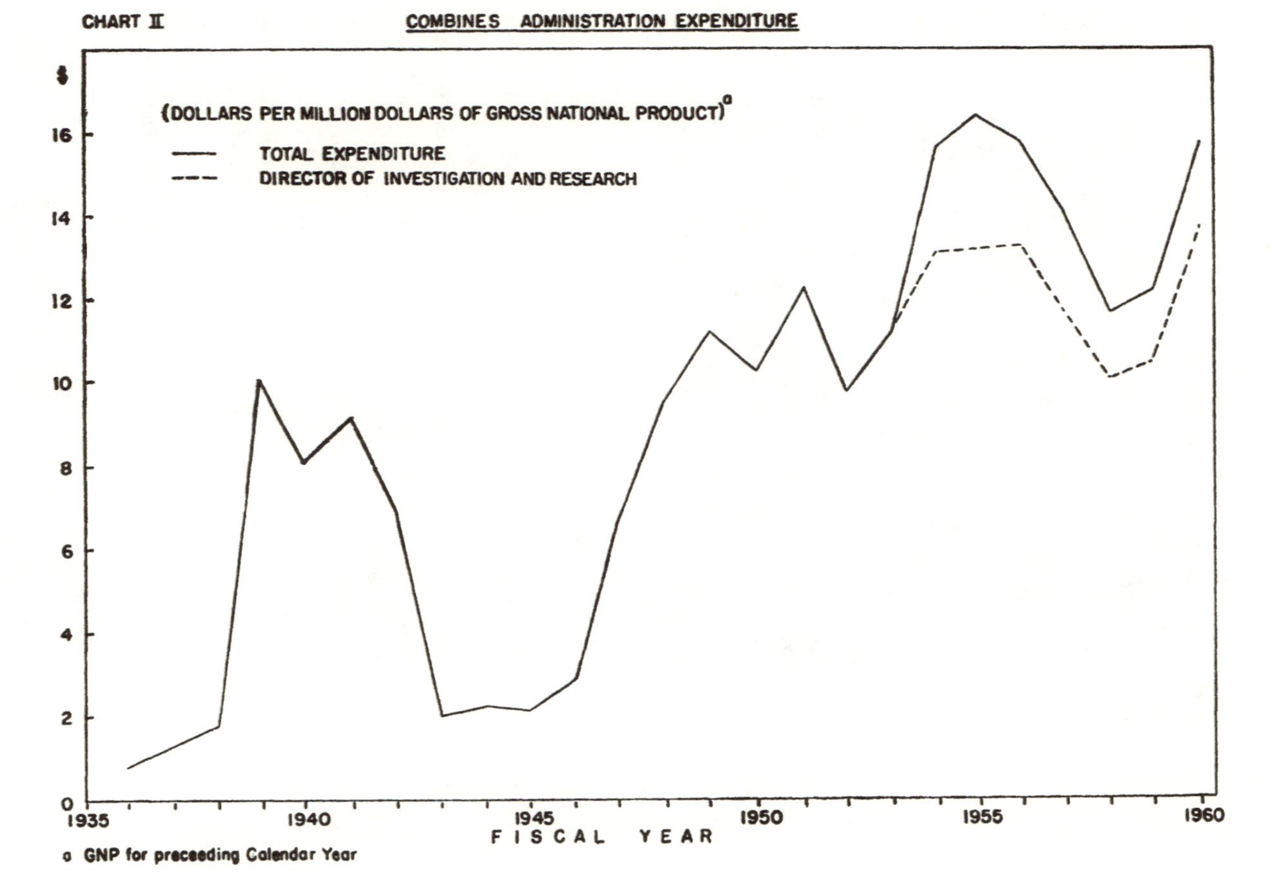

machinery, thirty-three reports appeared. Thus the average annual rate of output of published reports rose from less than one in the thirties, to two in the late forties, and more than four after the revision of the act.

When viewed against the background of the great increase in general economic activity, however, the increase in the volume of anti-combines work looks less spectacular. The rate at which investigations are undertaken increased greatly, but so did the number of situations that should be investigated, so that the relative effectiveness of the investigative machinery rose by much less than the increased expenditure might suggest. The figures on combines expenditure per million dollars of Gross National Product suggest that, in relation to the "need," combines expenditure did rise somewhat with the establishment of the new machinery, but that later it dropped, so that by 1958/9 expenditure per million dollars of Gross National Product was below the level of 1950/1. The considerably higher expenditure of 1959/60 was still below the peak levels of 1953/4 to 1955/6 in relation to the Gross National Product.

By relating combines expenditures to the Gross National Product, a rough comparison can also be made between expenditures in Canada and in the United States. As a proportion of the Gross National Product, combines expenditures in Canada, in fiscal years 1957/8 and 1958/9, were of a similar order of magnitude to anti-trust expenditures in the United States, but somewhat lower. Canadian figures for these two years were $12 per million dollars of Gross National Product (Table III) while anti-trust expenditures in the United States were $14 and $16 per million dollars of Gross National Product.[4] In judging the significance of these figures the following considerations are relevant. Anti-trust expenditure in the United States has frequent-

---

[4] Calculated from data on expenditures of the Antitrust Division, Department of Justice, and expenditures of the Federal Trade Commission on Anti-Monopoly Work, given in the *Budget of the United States Government for the Fiscal Year ending June 30, 1960*, (Washington, 1960) pp. 169, 734. Gross National Product from *Business Statistics 1959* (Washington, 1959) and *Survey of Current Business*, October 1960. Since federal expenditure figures are for twelve months ending in June, Gross National Product figures used are averages for adjacent years.

COMBINES ADMINISTRATION EXPENDITURE

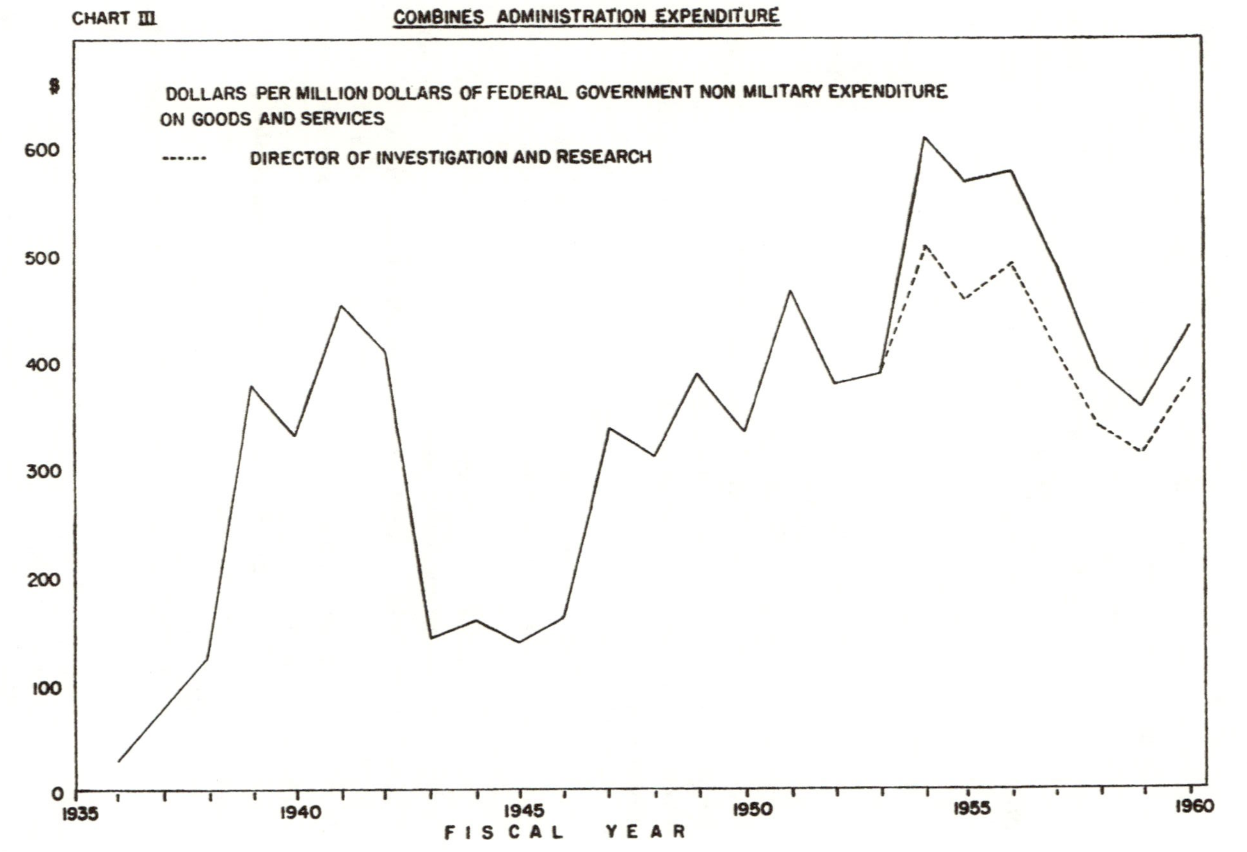

ly been criticized as being inadequate.[5] Yet in the United States there has been a great deal of action in types of cases that have not been effectively tackled in Canada. In particular, cases involving mergers, single firm monopolies, and price discrimination have received much attention. Moreover, it is reasonable to assume that in anti-combines activity as in other spheres there are "economies of large scale," so that United States activity is probably more effective, per dollar of expenditure, than in Canada. Finally, the "need" for anti-combines activity "per dollar of G.N.P." is most likely greater in Canada than in the United States owing to the much greater prevalence of high concentration of market control.[6]

The funds assigned to combines investigation by government policy, as a proportion of total federal non-military expenditures on goods and services, have followed a similar trend. The "pre-war" peak in fiscal year 1940/1 was exceeded ten years later, and the proportion of non-military expenditure devoted to combines investigation rose still higher after the establishment of the new administrative machinery. After 1955/6 it declined, however, so that in 1959 it was lower than in almost any other post-war year and, indeed, lower than in 1938/9. The 1960 level is much higher but is still below the levels of 1940/1, 1950/1, and 1953/4 to 1956/7.

Table IV and Chart IV show the two major components of anti-combines expenditure: salaries and fees. The bulk of the fees are those paid to legal counsel retained to fight combines cases in the courts, but the figures also include small sums paid to consultants, accountants, special assistants, witnesses, and stenographic reporters.

The fluctuations in total expenditure are traceable to the fluctuations in fees. Salaries rose continuously in the period reviewed (in money terms) except from 1938/9 to 1945/6 and again from 1949/50 to 1950/1 when they were nearly unchanged.

---

[5] See, for example, Corwin D. Edwards, *Maintaining Competition* (New York, 1949) pp. 292-8. While this comment is not very recent, anti-trust expenditures as a proportion of the Gross National Product were considerably higher when he wrote than in 1958 and 1959.

[6] See G. Rosenbluth, *Concentration in Canadian Manufacturing Industries* (Princeton, 1957), chap. IV.

TABLE IV
COMBINES EXPENDITURE, MAIN ITEMS

Fiscal year	Total $000	Salaries $000	Fees $000
1936	3.4	2.4	—
1937			
1938	14.6	10.6	2.5
1939	52.5	18.7	16.4
1940	45.3	19.1	22.3
1941	61.8	20.6	38.8
1942	57.5	22.4	32.3
1943	23.4	20.3	2.2
1944	25.2	21.3	2.3
1945	24.9	21.2	2.4
1946	34.6	22.3	8.8
1947	77.6	57.7	10.8
1948	124.8	63.9	47.4
1949	169.4	86.3	65.0
1950	168.8	104.1	44.8
1951	221.1	103.5	94.9
1952	205.8	115.5	75.9
1953	267.0	154.8	72.9
1954	393.7	203.6	134.1
1955	407.5	224.3	124.9
1956	426.5	240.2	125.6
1957	427.9	268.6	102.9
1958	372.9	279.2	56.3
1959	394.2	287.3	66.2
1960	541.9	305.4	177.6

Source: *Public Accounts.*

The "pre-war" peak in total expenditure, in 1940/1, and subsequent decline clearly reflect the abrupt changes in fees. Similarly the decline from 1950/1 to 1951/2 in total expenditures, in the period between the resignation of Mr. McGregor and the revision of the legislation, reflects a sudden decline in fees, which continued to 1952/3. Fees reached a peak in 1953/4 and then fell rapidly, but there was a sharp rise in 1959/60, mainly owing to

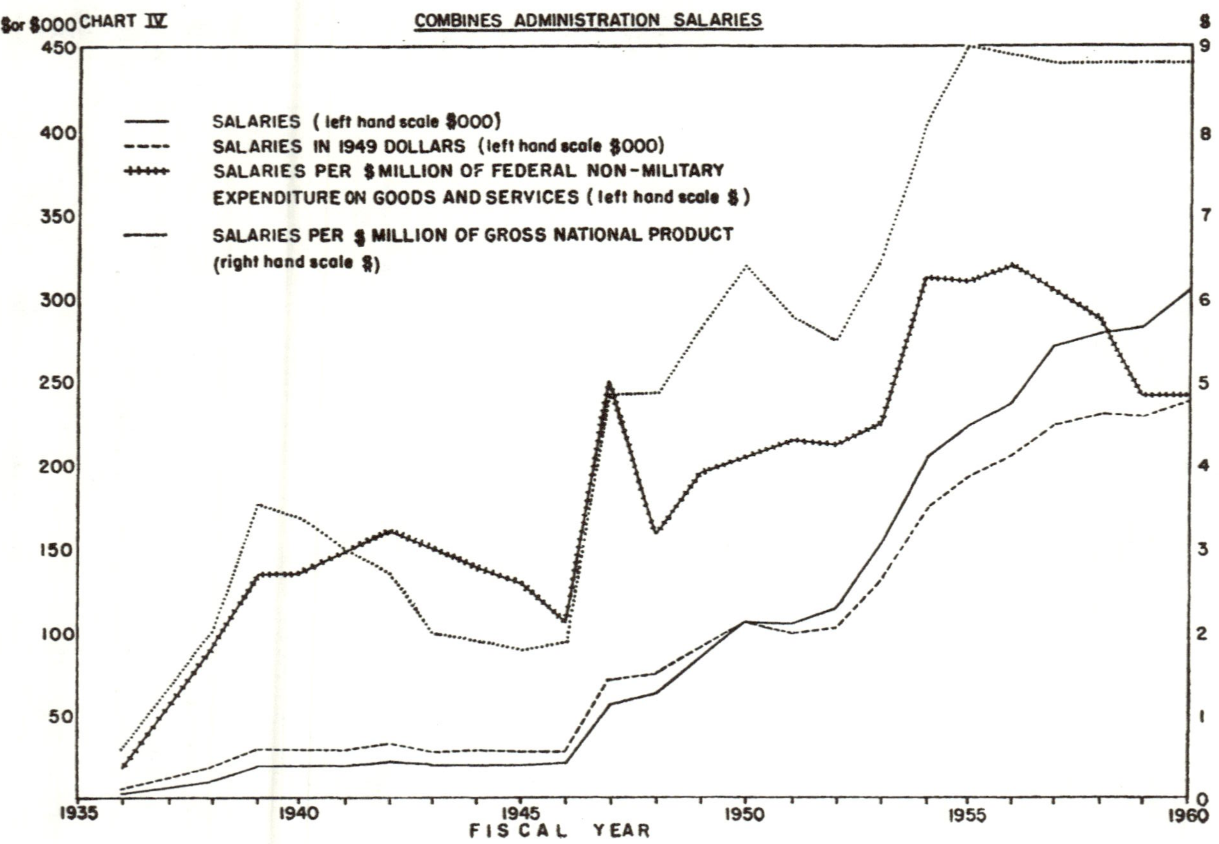
$or $000 CHART IV
COMBINES ADMINISTRATION SALARIES
SALARIES (left hand scale $OOO)
SALARIES IN 1949 DOLLARS (left hand scale $OOO)
SALARIES PER $ MILLION OF FEDERAL NON-MILITARY EXPENDITURE ON GOODS AND SERVICES (left hand scale $)
SALARIES PER $ MILLION OF GROSS NATIONAL PRODUCT (right hand scale $)
FISCAL YEAR

the Canadian Breweries case. This increase is the chief reason for the striking increase in total expenditures in 1959/60.

While fees reflect the greatly fluctuating burden of prosecutions, therefore, salaries alone are a better indication of the steady trend in investigation and reporting activity. Salaries in constant dollars, as well as in relation to the Gross National Product and federal non-military expenditure, are shown in Table V. All of these indicators show a significantly higher level of activity after the war, and all show a further rise after the introduction of the new administrative machinery. Since the middle fifties, however, salaries have declined somewhat, both as a proportion of the Gross National Product and in relation to other federal non-military expenditures.

The number of employees of the combines branch rose from 34 in 1951/2 to 50 in 1953/4 (43 for the Director of Investigation and Research) and has remained at about that level. The increase was mainly in non-professional staff. The number of professional employees rose from 13 in 1951/2 to 21 in 1952/3 (18 for the Director's office) and ranged from 18 to 20 thereafter (16-17 for the Director's office).[7]

It may be concluded that with the establishment of the new machinery the resources devoted to the administration of the act increased, as did the amount of activity under the act. Subsequent expansion, however, did not keep pace with the growth of the economy and of other government activities. If legal work in connection with prosecutions is taken into account, combines activity, considered in relation to both the Gross National Product and total government activity, was lower in 1958/9 than in the last years of the preceding administrative system, but rose sharply in 1959/60. If the fluctuating level of legal activity is left out of account, it is significant that the size of the professional staff has not increased since 1952/3 and total staff since 1953/4. The total resources devoted to anti-combines work are very small when compared with other government activities. In the next chapter we shall investigate whether they are also small in relation to the need.

---

[7] *Annual Reports*, 1952-9.

TABLE V
COMBINES INVESTIGATION SALARIES [1]

Fiscal year [2]	Salaries $000	Salaries in 1949 dollars [3] $000	Salaries per $ million of Gross National Product [4]	Salaries per $ million of federal non-military expenditure on goods and services [4]
1936	2	4	0.6	18
1937				
1938	11	17	2.0	90
1939	19	29	3.5	134
1940	19	30	3.4	134
1941	21	31	3.0	147
1942	22	32	2.7	159
1943	20	28	2.0	150
1944	21	29	1.9	139
1945	21	28	1.8	124
1946	22	30	1.9	108
1947	58	75	4.9	251
1948	64	75	4.9	159
1949	86	89	5.7	197
1950	104	104	6.4	205
1951	104	101	5.8	214
1952	116	102	5.5	212
1953	155	133	6.5	225
1954	204	176	8.1	312
1955	224	193	9.0	311
1956	240	206	8.9	320
1957	269	227	8.8	305
1958	279	229	8.8	290
1959	283	230	8.8	242
1960	305	241	8.8	243

[1] "Salaries" and "Full Time Positions" listed under the Combines Investigation Act in the Public Accounts of Canada.

[2] Twelve months ending March 31 of the year shown.

[3] As in Table III, note 3.

[4] As in Table III, note 4.

Sources: as in Table III.

7. Scope of Activities Under the Combines Act

A COMPARISON of economic areas to which the combines machinery has been effectively applied with areas in which monopolistic practices or undue economic concentration are known or likely to prevail is made in this chapter. Such an investigation presents formidable difficulties but must be attempted. Without it there is no answer to a basic question in the history of combines administration: does anti-combines activity in Canada represent a serious attempt to influence the structure and functioning of the Canadian economy, or is it essentially a political gesture designed to meet the demands of voters while leaving the structure and practices of business substantially unaffected? The importance of this question for a proper evaluation of the role of the Combines Act in the Canadian economy is evident.

This examination of the relative importance of areas to which the combines legislation has or has not been applied will not in itself indicate the legislation's effectiveness, but it will supply necessary basic information. Spotty enforcement of prohibitions is sometimes defended on the grounds that making an example of a few cases is a sufficient deterrent. But is enforcement sufficiently frequent to have this deterrent effect or is it so unusual as to lead to widespread violations and the impression that the rules are not expected to be observed? In making such a judgment, we must take into account not only the frequency but also the character of enforcement. For example, if convictions carry small fines and no safeguards against repetition of the offence, they may not even act as a deterrent for the convicted party.

In listing cases effectively dealt with by the combines machinery, we are necessarily confined to the published sources: judicial decisions, the reports of the Restrictive Trade Practices Commission, and the annual reports of the director. The latter contain accounts of cases in which monopolistic practices were abandoned after preliminary enquiry without the issue being brought before the Restrictive Trade Practices Commission. Such cases are not numerous. There is no record, however, of cases in which planned or contemplated restrictive arrangements were abandoned after consultation with the director's office. It must be assumed that there are such cases, since consultation is encouraged by the director. Moreover, there cannot be any record of the number and importance of cases in which, even without consultation, the existence of the combines legislation prevented restrictive arrangements that would otherwise have taken place. These considerations must be taken into account in the evaluation of our data.

The list of situations not effectively dealt with by the combines machinery is based on a variety of sources, including Commission reports and the annual reports of the director. In compiling such a list the investigator must, of course, use his own judgment about the type of industry structure or behaviour that calls for action, and in the cases where some action was taken under the combines legislation he must use his own judgment as to whether the action was effective. A list of this kind is bound to be incomplete and to contain speculative and controversial decisions. We cannot reasonably expect to do more than offer a sample of these situations.

A special difficulty arises where effective action appears to have been taken, in the sense that a conviction was secured, yet there is reason to believe that monopolistic practices or structures have not been eliminated. These cases have been included in the list of those "effectively dealt with," except for a few cases where strong and specific contrary evidence was available. The lists are thus biased by including too many cases among those "effectively handled."

Further difficulties surround the question of how to measure the importance of a particular market in which monopolistic structures or practices are found. Apart from the problems of defining the geographical extent of the market and the range of firms, commodities, or services that should be included, there is the problem of measuring its significance in comparison with that of other markets. The total value of sales would seem an appropriate measure, but when different periods of time are compared a correction must be made for differences in the price level and in the total size of the economy. We correct for both these factors by expressing the size of each market as a proportion of the current Gross National Product. Moreover, as far as possible, all market sizes are measured in the same year, 1956. Market size cannot be measured accurately but must be estimated by techniques involving, in some cases, bold assumptions, cumbersome calculations, and very rough guesses.

It has also been necessary to set a given period of time for our comparison. We are interested in the period 1952 to 1960. We have included in the list of cases "effectively handled" some that were terminated after 1952, even though the investigations, and in some cases even the reports, belong to the preceding period. We have also included cases terminated after the 1960 revision of the legislation, if the reports were issued before that time. We have listed separately cases on which final action had not been completed at the time of writing.

Our data are presented below in tabular form, and the supporting material is given in the appendices at the end of the chapter. Notes on the factors considered in classifying the tabulated cases are in appendix I. Appendix II gives the sources and methods for the estimation of relative market size.

TABLE VI
MONOPOLISTIC SITUATIONS EFFECTIVELY HANDLED BY COMBINES MACHINERY
A. *Cases in Which Court Issued Restraining Order* *

Industry	Date of report	Relative Size of Market ($ per $000 of G.N.P.)
Rubber	1952	11.90
Electrical wire and cable	1953	6.17
Coarse papers, B.C.	1953	0.29
Wire fencing	1954	0.23
Retail coal sales, Timmins	1954	0.04
Asphalt roofing	1955	1.54
Transmission & conveyor equipment	1956	1.83
Retail coal sales, Winnipeg	1956	1.24
Quilting	1956	0.12
Boxboard	1956	2.21
Metal culverts	1957	0.61
Purchased pulpwood, eastern Canada	1958	0.83
Electrical contractors, Ont.	1959	2.29
TOTAL		29.32

* All these cases involve price agreement or restriction of entry.

B. *Cases in Which Monopoly Exposed in Commission Report But Court Action Not Required* *

Industry	Date of report	Relative size of market ($ per $000 of G.N.P.)	Remarks
Television sets, Toronto	1954	0.002	resale price maintenance
Flue-cured tobacco, Ont.	1956	1.87	collusion
TOTAL		1.87	

* These are cases in which court action has not been undertaken and, in the authors' judgment, is not required.

*C. Monopolistic Situations in Which Convictions Have Been
Secured without Restraining Order*

Industry or firm	Date of report	Relative size of market ($ per $000) of G.N.P.)	Remarks
Optical goods	1948	1.54	monopoly, patent control
Bread, western Canada	1948	2.33	collusion
Flat glass	1949	1.52	collusion
China and earthenware, Parsons-Steiner	1954	n.a.	resale price maintenance
Household supplies, Chicoutimi	1954	n.a.	resale price maintenance
Appliances, Moffats	1955	n.a.	resale price maintenance
TOTAL	More than 5.39		

(n.a.: not available)

TABLE VII

MONOPOLISTIC SITUATIONS NOT EFFECTIVELY HANDLED BY COMBINES MACHINERY

A. Cases Mentioned in Reports, But No Effective Action Taken

Industry	Date of report	Relative size of market ($ per $000 of G.N.P.)	Remarks
Dental supplies	1947	0.41	collusion
Matches	1949	0.27	monopoly
Flour milling	1949	7.37	collusion
Fine papers	1952	2.27	collusion
Gasoline, Vancouver area	1954	1.13	collusion
Brewing	1955	7.18	merger
Sugar, western Canada	1957	0.74	merger
Yeast	1958	3.82	merger
Zinc oxide	1958	0.10	merger, price discrimination, and predatory price cutting
Zinc	1958	0.68	monopoly
TOTAL		23.97	

B. Selected Cases Mentioned in Annual Reports of Director of Investigation and Research, with No Report by Commission

Industry	Date of annual report	Relative size of market ($ per $000 of G.N.P.)	Remarks
Household appliances, Winnipeg	1955	n.a.	refusal to sell
Shipping rates, Nfld.	1955	n.a.	collusion
Milk, Vancouver area	1955	0.33	collusion
Fertilizer, eastern Canada	1955	1.02	collusion or price leadership
Cigarettes, Toronto	1955	1.11	collusion
Electrical equipment	1956, 1957	8.70	collusion
Cement	1957	2.61	price discrimination
Storage batteries	1958	0.91	merger
Molasses	1958	0.06	monopoly, restriction of entry, discrimination
Paper bags, western Canada	1958	0.20	merger
Telephones, B.C.	1958	1.23	monopoly
Television sets, Ont.	1958	n.a.	price discrimination
Steel scrap, Vancouver area	1959	n.a.	monopoly, price discrimination
Pacific westbound shipping	1959	n.a.	collusion
Sand and gravel	1959	n.a.	collusion
Specialty foods, P.Q.	1959	n.a.	restriction of entry
Cigarettes, northern Ont.	1959	n.a.	restriction of entry
TOTAL		more than 16.17	

(n.a.: not available)

C. Examples of Industries and Products Where Concentration
Is High and Business Policies Should Be Investigated

Industry	Relative market size ($ per $000 of G.N.P.)
Agricultural implements	3.8
Electrical apparatus and supplies	
(excluding heavy machinery, wire & cable)	21.3
Primary iron and steel	22.8
Primary non-ferrous metals	
(excluding zinc)	42.2
Automobiles	32.7
Chartered banks	10.4
Grocery chain mergers	36.2
TOTAL	169.0

The tabulations can be summarized as follows:

SUMMARY

	Relative size of market ($ per $000 of G.N.P.)
I. Situations effectively handled	
I A	29.3
I B	1.9
I C	5.4
TOTAL, Group I	36.6
II. Examples of situations not effectively handled	
II A	23.9
II B	More than 16.2
II C	169.0
TOTAL, Group II	More than 209.1

These illustrative estimates, rough though they are, suggest that combines enforcement could be more effective. Along with the relative neglect of research (chapter IV) and the low level of expenditures (chapter VI), they suggest that the policy of successive administrations has been to keep anti-combines activity at a low level.

It has been suggested, however, that combines administration in itself may have a substantial preventive effect. Clearly the deterrent role of combines administration must be a matter of speculation, but some relevant guesses can be made.

It is probable that the Combines Investigation Act has had some preventive influence in the area of price agreements. Nearly all the convictions have been in this type of case, and the records of judicial interpretations make the law's implications clear.[1] Businessmen who consult the combines branch about arrangements involving an element of price agreements presumably can get a clear answer.

Nevertheless, there is good reason to believe that price agreements persist on a fairly wide scale. There have been major cases of price agreements that were exposed in combines reports, but, for one reason or another, not prosecuted or not successfully prosecuted. The Flour Milling and Dental Supplies cases are outstanding examples.[2] In other cases it appears that convictions and fines have not eliminated the monopolistic arrangement. The Fine Papers case is only one example. All these cases must encourage the view that evasion of the law is possible.

Moreover, certain types of cases do not seem to attract prosecution. Since the government dropped the Vancouver Gasoline

[1] This statement refers to the period preceding the new amendments of 1960 (see chapter vIII). The rewording of the legislation relating to price agreements raises new problems of interpretation and will have to be clarified by judicial decisions.

Before the 1960 amendments, most price agreements were prosecuted under section 411 of the Criminal Code and judicial decisions left little doubt that it prohibited price agreements *per se*. The Vancouver Gasoline case, however, was prosecuted under section 32 of the Combines Investigation Act and the 1956 decision of the British Columbia Court of Appeal suggested that "specific detriment" must be proven to establish illegality of an agreement. (*Regina* v. *Morrey et al.*, (1957) 6 D.L.R. (2d) 114). Subsequent *Annual Reports* of the director refer to this conflict of interpretations. (See, for example, *Annual Report*, 1958, p. 8.) Yet the government chose to drop the case, though given the opportunity for a new trial in which the Appeal Court's interpretation could have been reviewed. (See appendix I.)

[2] See chapter II and appendix I. See appendix I also for discussions of all further cases mentioned in the text.

case (apparently because it did not wish to subject the small businessmen concerned to "undue hardship" by further court proceedings[3]), it left the impression that it was willing to be lenient towards combines among local groups of small retailers. At the other end of the scale, informal price agreement on an "oligopoly" (a small group of sellers in control of a market) is likely to escape prosecution because of the difficulty of finding proof specific enough for criminal proceedings. In most cases brought into court, the Crown has relied largely on documentary evidence. Prosecutions have therefore been for violations where the number of firms is large enough to require written records of price agreements. Agreements made by telephone are difficult to detect and even more difficult to prosecute, and the director, in his annual reports, mentions many cases of "possible" agreement that were dropped because of the difficulty of securing evidence. Numerous identical bids on public tenders have been mentioned in the press, yet have escaped prosecution.

Price agreements in service industries are not covered by the act, and price agreements in industries subject to some degree of government regulation appear to be immune, even if no effective price regulation exists. Agreements among the banks have not been attacked, although it is doubtful if they are exempt from the act.

The combines machinery might also be applied to mergers. Several merger cases have been investigated, but the results imply that no merger short of complete monopoly should be deterred by the present legislation. In a number of cases involving significant lessening of competition, proceedings have been dropped by the director (e.g., Batteries) or the Commission has recommended no further action (e.g. Yeast, Zinc Oxide). Of the three cases that have been in court (Matches, Beer, Sugar), the first led to a fine, but no change in industry structure, and the other two to acquittals.[4] Recent decisions have interpreted the law to mean that only a merger which eliminates virtually

---

[3] *Annual Report,* 1957, p. 25.

[4] One of the grounds for acquittal cited by the court in the Canadian Breweries case was that provincial liquor control boards have the power to regulate beer prices.

all competition in a previously competitive situation, or which results in demonstrably inordinate prices or profits, would be held illegal.[5]

Price discrimination (discrimination by one seller between different buyers with respect to price or terms of sale), is widely practised in Canada, in spite of a clause apparently directed against it in the anti-combines legislation. The clause is not considered enforceable because it forbids discrimination "in respect of a sale of goods of like quality and quantity"; thus minor differences in any quantity sold could be used as a defence. The 1960 amendments to the act have not altered this situation, though they have prohibited discrimination in the form of "promotional allowances."

The law against resale price maintenance introduced in 1951 has probably promoted competition in the sale of automobiles and appliances appreciably. It does not appear to have altered the operations of drug stores, the traditional stronghold of resale price maintenance.[6]

In summary, the anti-combines legislation has undoubtedly somewhat discouraged collusive pricing policies and resale price maintenance. A wide range of price agreements, however, is not attacked by the combines machinery, and in other areas, notably mergers and price discrimination, it is quite ineffective.

On the whole, therefore, the application of combines machinery has been very limited. While stressing this, we shall not attempt to assess how far each of the parties concerned — the cabinets that approve the legislation and amendments, the ministers of justice who make policy decisions within the framework of the legislation, the director, the Commission, the counsel retained to conduct prosecutions, and the judges who interpret the law — is

---

[5] *Regina* v. *the British Columbia Sugar Refining Company Limited et al.,* Manitoba Court of Queen's Bench, August 8, 1960.

The result of this decision is already evident in the acquisition of Calgary Breweries by Canadian Breweries and the merger of the Imperial and Commerce Banks, both announced early in 1961. The latter was specifically sanctioned by the government.

[6] The 1960 amendments have, however, introduced new "defences" for persons accused of resale price maintenance, which, in the view of informed commentators, will make the law almost impossible to enforce. (See chapter viii.)

responsible for such a state of affairs. In some respects, such an assessment is impossible for an outside investigator, since he cannot, for example, have adequate knowledge of the relations of the minister of justice with his Cabinet colleagues on the one hand and the director on the other. In other respects, the task is not impossible but is beyond the resources, in time and money, of most individual research workers. For example, the recent judicial decisions in the Beer and Sugar cases mean that the present legislation is ineffective in preventing mergers. Some impression of the role of the prosecution in the formation of these decisions could be gained by studying the complete court records. But these records can only be obtained at considerable expense, and they are so voluminous that their study would take a great deal of time.

However, in more than a technical a sense, ultimate responsibility for the scope of anti-combines activity rests with the Cabinet. It selects the director and the Commission, determines their budgets, and can issue directives that govern their work. It selects prosecuting counsel and is responsible for their instructions.[7] It can initiate changes in the legislation to meet needs revealed by judicial interpretation. If the application of the combines machinery has been very limited, this state of affairs reflects the policy of successive governments, both Liberal and Conservative.

APPENDIX I

Notes on the Classification of Tabulated Cases

Table VI B

Television sets. A localized instance of resale price maintenance by R.C.A., which did not, apparently, have a general policy of enforcing resale prices.

---

[7] When there is a change of government, the new government must, of course, continue the director and commissioners at least until their terms run out or there is a resignation. They can, and do, however, change prosecuting counsel on a combines case in preparation. This was done in the Canadian Breweries case.

Tobacco. The arrangement resembled that of statutory marketing boards and the Commission recommended that a statutory authority be established. In 1957 a marketing plan was adopted under the Farm Products Marketing Act of Ontario.

Table VII A

Dental supplies. A Combines Investigation Report completed in 1947 describes a combine among members of the Canadian Dental Trade Association, which included both manufacturers and dealers. A price fixing agreement among the dealers, who controlled most of the trade in dental supplies, was backed up by the policy of many Canadian and American manufacturers, who sold only to member dealers. No new dealers had been admitted to membership since 1928.

Members of the Association were prosecuted, but were acquitted on the ground that it had not been proven that the actions of corporate officers had been authorized by their corporations. This outcome led to the 1949 revision of the Combines Investigation Act.

No further action was taken against the combine and it is reported by dentists that the price fixing agreement is still in existence.

Matches. Following a report in 1949, the Eddy Match Company and its subsidiaries were convicted of maintaining a monopoly in the sale of matches, and fines totalling $85,000 plus costs were imposed. The company had long followed a general policy of acquiring new competitors after undermining their trade through unfair and discriminating sales practices.

The final court decision on appeal was made in 1953. "Consideration was then given, by the Department of Justice, to an application . . . for an order prohibiting the continuation or repetition of the offence, and dissolving the merger, trust, or monopoly. The conclusion was reached, however, that since the amendment to the Combines Investigation Act providing for such an order . . . had not come into force until after the conviction, such an application was not authorized by it." (*Annual Report,* 1955, p. 29)

The fines were low in relation to the company's profits, the monopoly was not dissolved, and no order of prohibition was issued. It may therefore be assumed that monopoly control continues.

The latest issue of the Dominion Bureau of Statistics' *General Review of the Manufacturing Industries of Canada,* covering the year 1957, indicates that book matches are produced by three or more concerns. Output of "matches, other" is, however, still not given, on the grounds that the commodity was reported by only one or two concerns. Statistics in the combines report on matches indicate that in 1948 the output of book matches was only about one-quarter that of wooden matches.

Flour milling. The Combines Investigation Report on the flour milling industry (1949), discussed in the text above, describes the operation of an elaborate price fixing agreement. However, no steps were taken by the government to prosecute the members of the combine or to assure its dissolution.

Fine papers. A report on a price fixing agreement covering fine papers was issued in 1952; the participating companies were subsequently convicted, fines were imposed, and a restraining order issued. The record outlined below suggests that, nevertheless, competition in the sale of fine papers was not restored.

In July 1960, Douglas Fisher, M.P., mentioned that the companies involved in the Fine Papers case had received letters from the Minister of Justice inviting them to show cause why their tariff protection should not be withdrawn (House of Commons, 3rd Session, 24th Parliament, 1960; Standing Committee on Banking & Commerce, *Minutes of Proceedings and Evidence*, no. 11, p. 658; see also no. 8, pp. 496-8). This action was taken under the section of the Combines Act which permits the Governor in Council to reduce or remove customs duty where this duty "facilitates" the disadvantage to the public arising from a combine. However, nothing further has been done, and tariff protection was not withdrawn.

Gasoline, Vancouver area. A report published in 1954 described a price fixing arrangement among retail gasoline dealers in Vancouver. Charges were laid under section 32 of the Combines Act, not section 411 of the Criminal Code as had been customary in price fixing cases. Convictions were obtained against a trade association and a number of individual dealers, but these convictions were quashed on appeal. The B.C. Court of Appeal argued that the doctrine that price fixing agreements are illegal *per se* did not apply when charges were brought under section 32 of the Combines Act, and that "specific detriment" to the public should have been proven (*Regina* v. *Morrey et al.*, 1957, 6 D.L.R. 2nd 114). "In view of the importance of the issues involved, to other cases" (*Annual Report*, 1956, p. 35, note 28), the Crown applied for leave to appeal to the Supreme Court, which was refused. Thereupon the government dropped the case, instead of proceeding with a new trial, as permitted by the appeal judgment. Nor did the Crown proceed with the trials of other defendants, which had been adjourned pending the outcome of the appeal. The reasons advanced for dropping the case (*Annual Report*, 1957, p. 25) were that, according to information received by the combines branch, the price fixing arrangement had been discontinued, and that further court proceedings would have caused "undue hardship" to the defendants.

A dissenting judgment on the appeal by Judge Davey reasoned that the Combines Act, properly construed, did hold price fixing agreements illegal *per se*. The government's application for leave to appeal to the Supreme Court was not, however, based on this dissent (see remarks by Kerwin C.J.C. in *Howard Smith Paper Mills Ltd. et al.* v. *the Queen,* Supreme Court of Canada, May 13, 1957).

If one may judge from the annual reports, this case appears to have altered the Director's view of the meaning of the combines legislation. Up to and including the report for the year ending March 1957, the reports state in the introductory section: "the mainstay of Canadian combines legislation is section 411 of the Criminal Code. Generally speaking this section forbids suppliers ... to arrange among themselves to eliminate competition over a substantial part of any market by limiting production, restricting distribution, or fixing prices." Section 32 of the Combines Act is described in these reports as differing only in that it also forbids "any 'merger, trust or monopoly', relating to a commodity, which has operated or is likely to operate to the detriment or against the interest of the public."

Subsequent reports no longer refer to section 411 as the "mainstay," emphasize its inclusion of the word "unduly," and refer to section 32 of the Combines Act as prohibiting a combination, as well as a merger or monopoly, only if it "has operated or is likely to operate to the detriment or against the interest of the public" (the interpretation rejected by Judge Davey). The reports go on to state: "the criteria which the courts will apply ... in determining when a practice or situation is detrimental to or against the interest of the public have not yet been clearly established. Some cases have appeared to assimilate the meaning of the words 'to the detriment or against the interest of the public' ... to that of 'unduly' in section 411 of the Criminal Code, but a recent case ... in the British Columbia Court of Appeal suggests a severer test involving proof of some immediate and specific harm." (*Annual Report*, 1958, pp. 7-8.) The reader is not informed that this is the Vancouver Gasoline case, which the government dropped.

Brewing. The report on beer (1955) described the extensive merger activities of Canadian Breweries Ltd. from the 1930's to the 1950's, which raised that company's share of total sales to over 60 per cent in Ontario, over 50 per cent in Ontario and Qubec combined, and well over 40 per cent for Canada. The evidence showed that these mergers had the object and effect of reducing competition.

A prosecution was launched after considerable delay, and in February 1960 the defendants were acquitted. A major factor in the decision was the judge's acceptance of the contention that beer prices in Ontario were under effective government control. On this point the evidence given in court for the defence differed from that given to the Commission. A second factor in the decision was that two other strong "competitors" — Molson's and Labatt's — remained in the industry. Evidence regarding collusion between Canadian Breweries and its "competitors" and evidence regarding the obstruction of entry were regarded as irrelevant to the decision.

Early in 1961 the further extension of Canadian Breweries' control by the acquisition of Calgary Breweries was announced in the press.

Sugar, western Canada. A report published in 1957 dealt with the acquisition of control by the British Columbia Sugar Refining Company over its sole western competitor, the Manitoba Sugar Company. The report showed that British Columbia Sugar Refining was the only supplier of sugar in British Columbia, Alberta, and most of Saskatchewan, while there had been active competition from Manitoba Sugar in parts of eastern Saskatchewan and in Manitoba. There was no price competition from eastern Canadian refineries because of general adherence to a basing point pricing system. In 1955 British Columbia Sugar Refining Company obtained a large minority block of Manitoba Sugar common shares and took over the management of the latter company, while plans were made to obtain majority control at a later date.

British Columbia Sugar Refining Company was prosecuted under the merger clause of the Combines Act and was acquitted in 1960. The judgment cited the Canadian Breweries case as a precedent.

Yeast. The report on yeast (1958) analyses the acquisition of Best Yeast Ltd. by Standard Brands Ltd. in 1955, which reduced the number of competitors in this industry from three to two. In 1954, before the acquisition, Standard Brands accounted for 75 per cent of total sales of yeast, Best for 9 per cent, and Lallemand, the remaining independent, for 16 per cent. In eastern Canada, Best's share was considerably greater and Lallemand's smaller (report, pp. 67-8). Lallemand's sales are concentrated in Quebec and constitute a very small factor in other areas.

The Commission stated: "We are concerned at the reduction in competition which has occured . . . by reason of the merger and the possibility of long term injury to the public which an approach to monopoly necessarily creates. The public interest would have been better served if a buyer (for Best) had been found who would have been a new entrant into the industry. . . . Such a buyer was not found . . . the Commission is not convinced that the public interest has been so affected as to justify recommending action to alter the integration of manufacturing operations which has been accomplished or the dissolution of the merger. If Best had been a more active competitor, or if its operations had been indicative of expansion, rather than decline, our view might well be different. . . .

. . . "Standard Brands not only should not be permitted to acquire its presently remaining competitor, but unless the structure of the industry is greatly altered it should not be permitted to acquire any new competitor that may enter the field." (p. 79)

Zinc oxide. The report on zinc oxide (1958) shows that the leading producer, Zinc Oxide Company of Canada, engaged in a price war with the object of eliminating one or both of its competitors, and was supported by discriminatory price concessions by its supplier of zinc, Hudson Bay Mining and Smelting Company. Ultimately it merged with the larger of its competitors, Durham Industries. Yet the report's recommendations deal only with price discrimination in zinc (and only as between zinc oxide producers) and suggest that consideration be given to the reduction of the customs duties on refined zinc.

Zinc. The report on zinc oxide mentions that there are only two domestic producers of zinc. The bulk of the output is exported, but domestic prices have been maintained at high levels in relation to delivered prices in export markets. Price discrimination in domestic sales was revealed. The recommendations in the report (see preceding paragraph) do not touch the basic monopoly structure and the discriminatory high domestic price.

Table VII B

Household appliances, Winnipeg. The *Annual Report,* 1954 (p. 36), records the complaint of a retailer of household appliances that wholesalers were refusing to supply as a result of pressure from other retailers. This pressure was because of price cutting by the retailer in question, which was combined with an unorthodox method of doing business.

Inquiry showed that the facts were as stated in the complaint, but the case was dropped because "the evidence ... did not go so far as to indicate either a combine or an infraction of section 34 relating to resale price maintenance" (p. 37).

Shipping rates, Newfoundland. The *Annual Report*, 1955 (p. 54), mentions complaints from "the provincial authorities of an Atlantic province" charging collusive rate fixing among shipping companies. The report states that "because of differences among the companies in ... conditions of shipment, it was found very difficult to make meaningful comparisons between their rates. While the possibility of some arrangements could not be dismissed, the rates of the shipping companies did not appear to be as high as the duly authorized "through" rates of the railways. The preliminary information gathered was sent to the provincial authorities for their further comments, but these had not been received at the end of the fiscal year." (p. 54)

Later reports do not refer to this case again, and so presumably the investigation has been dropped. The Board of Transport Commissioners does not regulate shipping rates between Newfoundland and mainland ports. The comparison with railway rates hardly seems pertinent, since a shipping monopoly would not maximize its profits unless its rates were lower than those of the railways.

Milk, Vancouver area. The *Annual Report*, 1955 (p. 47), describes an agreement among local dairies, which prevented hospitals and similar institutions from obtaining competitive tenders for the supply of milk.

While inquiries were being made by the combines branch, competitive tenders were received and the provincial Board authorized the importation of milk from other areas. "Having regard to this fact and the extent to which the whole situation was under the jurisdiction of the provincial authorities, it was felt that no purpose would be served in continuing the inquiry" (pp. 50-1). The combines branch thus deprived itself of the benefit of publicity which would have strengthened enforcement.

Fertilizer. The *Annual Report,* 1955 (p. 45), describes a complaint of a price fixing agreement covering mixed fertilizer in eastern Canada.

The preliminary inquiry indicated that list prices of major producers were substantially identical, but the report ascribes this to price leadership rather than collusion and states that "competition appeared to exist in seeking dealer accounts, in granting dealer and delivery discounts and in absorbing transportation costs" (p. 46).

Cigarettes, Toronto. The *Annual Report,* 1955 (p. 36), describes a complaint about a price agreement among tobacco wholesalers in Toronto fixing cigarette prices to retailers. Witnesses from the wholesalers stated "that there had been some conversation in the trade" about prices, but they denied collusion. The case was dropped "having regard to the inconclusive nature of the evidence and the unlikelihood that any further evidence could be obtained which ... would provide a basis for firm conclusions" (p. 37).

Electrical Equipment. The *Annual Reports,* 1957 (p. 27) and 1956 (p. 37), mention complaints of uniform tenders received by cities for supply of electrical equipment. Types of equipment are not specified (different types are involved in the two cases). Although evidence described in the reports strongly suggests collusion, the cases were not proceeded with because in one case "the information obtained was not strong enough" and in the other "information depended chiefly upon oral evidence which was not sufficiently precise."

Similar complaints have been reported in the press from time to time.

Cement. The *Annual Report,* 1957 (p. 29), describes the complaint of sales at unreasonably low prices by a large and long established manufacturer of a "building material" in the market areas of a new entrant in Quebec. There is little doubt that this account refers to the cement industry. Other complaints refer to refusal of the "long established" company to make "building material" available to the new entrant for a new plant it was building in Ontario and an attempt to "forestall" by tying up Ontario accounts on long-term contracts. The case was not proceeded with because "it appeared that the industry was competitive and that no abuse of a monopoly or quasi-monopoly position was involved."

Early in 1960 the press reported complaints by Toronto City Council of identical bids on tenders to supply cement.

Storage batteries. The *Annual Report,* 1958 (p. 25), refers to the merger of two leading manufacturers of storage batteries. There were only fifteen manufacturers altogether, and "preliminary study of the industry suggested that the new company formed by the merger would be the dominant producer and that detriment to the public might flow from the elimination of competition between the merging companies." However, no action was taken because further investigation "did not indicate that the new company arising from the merger would either substantially or completely control throughout any particular area in Canada or the country as a whole the manufacture and distribution of storage batteries, or that the merger would be likely to operate against the public interest" (p. 26).

The "presumption of innocence," which has its proper place in the courts, is here applied in the very early stages of investigation and a case is dropped because the first preliminary round of inquiries does not prove specific injury to the public. Criteria of this kind have minimized the number of cases that are investigated at all carefully.

Molasses. The *Annual Report*, 1958 (p. 23), describes the attempt of a new entrant to break into the business of importing molasses from the British West Indies into eastern Canada, which was a single-firm monopoly. The monopolist firm also monopolized the purchase of blackstrap in the West Indies through its control of transport and storage facilities. Among the practices used to hamper the new entrant, the report mentions attempts to prevent it from obtaining shipping and storage facilities, the tying of producers' supplies in the West Indies, price competition which, according to the complainant, amounted to sale at unreasonably low prices in order to drive the new entrant out of business.

Independent information indicates that the "attempt to prevent it from obtaining shipping and storage facilities" included the denial of bulk-loading facilities controlled by the monopolist in the West Indies, successful pressure on a city council, through one of the councillors, to cancel a lease of city land for storage tanks used by the new entrant, and pressure on a Canadian shipping company to deny lake tanker facilities to transport the molasses to Toronto.

This is a case in which the single firm monopoly might well have been attacked by tariff changes since the existing tariff structure favours imports from the British West Indies.

The investigation was dropped because, "while the activities of the company complained about had at times approached the boundary of behaviour contrary to the Act, the evidence, upon the whole, was not clear cut or extensive enough ... nor was it believed that further inquiry would disclose any further material of significance" (p. 25). The Commission concurred in the decision to drop the case.

Paper bags. The *Annual Report*, 1958 (p. 21), refers to the acquisition of one leading paper bag manufacturer by another in 1955. The companies concerned, as mentioned in press reports, were the Crown-Zellerbach interests and B. C. Bertram, an independent paper bag manufacturer in British Columbia.

This acquisition followed the exposure, in the report of the Combines Investigation Commission on coarse paper, of a collusive combine covering paper bags, in which Bertram, then the major bag producer, and Pacific Mills, the Crown-Zellerbach subsidiary, participated. The acquisition therefore appears to be an example of the practice, frequently discussed in the United States literature, of replacing a collusive agreement by a merger.

The reasons given in the *Annual Report* (p. 23) for dropping the case were:

(*a*) "The fact that the acquired company was dependent, for its kraft paper, upon the firm engaged in the manufacture of grocery bags, and was likely to continue to be so dependent upon one or another such firm, doubtless places a significant limit on the ability ... of the acquired company to give effective competition."

(*b*) "The entry ... of a new company at about the same time ... might be expected to afford customers an alternative source of supply at least as good as existed before the merger."

(*c*) "Because of the dispersal of the acquired company's assets ... it would be difficult to secure an order ... severing such assets from those of the acquiring company."

The following comments are pertinent:

(*a*) With the expansion of the industry new entrants into the production of kraft paper were to be expected, and, in fact, it was known at the time of the investigation that a new firm was entering this business. Moreover, a lowering of the tariff would introduce import competition.

(*b*) This line of reasoning would deprive the public of the benefit of increased competition that is normally to be expected as the market grows and new firms enter.

(*c*) The fact that dissolution would be "difficult" seems an inadequate reason for not trying.

B.C. Telephone Co. The *Annual Report*, 1955 (p. 38ff.), describes a complaint that "a local telephone company" was buying equipment from related companies at excessive monopoly prices, resulting in an enhancement of telephone rates and in the funnelling of profits from a company regulated by the Board of Transport Commissioners to an unregulated company.

Although the preliminary information obtained supported the complaint, the inquiry was discontinued, and no clear reason was given in the *Annual Report* (see especially p. 44). This decision was to be reviewed if, at any time, "the situation appeared in a different light, or new facts appeared."

Television sets, Ontario. The *Annual Report*, 1958 (p. 28), mentions a complaint by a dealer that he had been discriminated against in price by the manufacturer of a well known brand of sets. After preliminary investigation the case was dropped because the information "was inconclusive and conflicting" (pp. 28-9).

Steel scrap, Vancouver area. The *Annual Report,* 1959 (p. 26), mentions a complaint that a Vancouver steel mill was paying higher prices for scrap to three large dealers than to smaller competitors. The mill enjoyed a monopoly position.

Inquiry was abandoned after scrap exports were freed from restrictions, thus destroying the firm's monopoly position, and the firm reported it would follow a different policy if it again enjoyed a monoply position.

Pacific shipping. The *Annual Report,* 1959 (p. 31), mentions complaints about activities of a United States-based shipping cartel, controlling rates from Pacific coast ports in the United States and Canada to Asian countries in the northern hemisphere.

The inquiry was dropped because a second inquiry concerning Atlantic shipping conferences was initiated and "simultaneous conduct of the two inquiries would explore substantially the same issues." The termination of the inquiry was "subject to re-opening should the circumstances later warrant such action" (p. 32).

Sand and gravel. Reports on local price agreements in the supply of sand and gravel are contained in the annual reports for 1958 (p. 26) and 1959 (p. 35). In one case the inquiry was stopped because the agreement was reported to have been discontinued. In the second case the evidence was found to be "insufficient" to warrant the submission of a Statement of Evidence.

Specialty food products. The *Annual Report,* 1959 (p. 36), mentions a complaint by a wholesaler of refusal to supply on the part of manufacturers, owing to pressure from other wholesalers. Inquiry was discontinued because "the evidence was not strong enough." The report adds: "This is a typical example of the restrictive behaviour that has been found to ensue, either without agreement or without likelihood of proving it, when the number of leading manufacturers in an industry is very small" (p. 36).

Cigarettes, northern Ontario. The *Annual Report,* 1959 (p. 36), mentions a complaint by a wholesaler of local price cutting by other wholesalers as well as interference with his supply. The inquiry indicated the existence of these practices, but the evidence was not considered sufficient for successful prosecution, and so the inquiry was discontinued.

Table VII C

Agricultural implements. According to J. D. Woods and Gordon Ltd.,[1] four companies account for 95 per cent of output, as follows: Massey-Harris-Ferguson, over 50 per cent; International Harvester, 25-30 per cent; Cockshutt, 15 per cent; John Deere, smaller percentage.

According to W. G. Phillips,[2] "price competition has been inactive in most of the industry's history."

Electrical apparatus and supplies. Concentration data for individual products, 1954, show that, with few exceptions, eight firms account for four-fifths or more of each product and four firms for more than three-fifths.[3] Six firms account for about four-fifths of the market for electronic equipment.[4]

A patent pool has been used to impose a private ban on imports of radios, television sets, and other electronic equipment.[5] This practice has become the basis of United States anti-trust action against the parent companies of the leading Canadian producers.

Primary iron and steel industry. The four largest producers — Dosco, Stelco, Algoma, and Dofasco — produce all the pig iron, over 90 per cent of steel ingots and castings, and nearly 90 per cent of the rolling mill products. Base prices are generally higher than those in the Unites States.[6] According to Reynolds, "most of the major products [of the iron and steel industry] would probably fall either under 'monopoly' or under 'price agreement'."[7]

Primary non-ferrous metals. High concentration in the smelting and refining of non-ferrous metals is well known. There is, for example, one producer in the case of aluminum and lead, two for nickel and zinc, five for copper. Monopolistic pricing and price discrimination in the case of zinc were indicated in the report of the Restrictive

---

[1] *The Canadian Agricultural Machinery Industry* (Royal Commission on Canada's Economic Prospects, Ottawa, 1956), p. 34.

[2] *The Agricultural Implement Industry in Canada* (Toronto, 1956), p. 162 and chap. 9.

[3] C. L. Barber, *The Canadian Electrical Manufacturing Industry* (Royal Commission on Canada's Economic Prospects, Ottawa, 1956), p. 29.

[4] Canadian Business Service Ltd., *The Electronics Industry in Canada* (Royal Commission on Canada's Economic Prospects, Ottawa, 1956), p. 25.

[5] *Ibid.*, pp. 24-5.

[6] Bank of Nova Scotia, *The Canadian Primary Iron and Steel Industry* (Royal Commission on Canada's Economic Prospects, Ottawa, 1956), pp. 2, 80, 81.

[7] L. G. Reynolds, *The Control of Competition in Canada* (Cambridge, 1940), p. 9.

Trade Practices Commission on zinc oxide. The other primary producers have not been investigated.

Motor vehicles. The three major producers, General Motors, Ford, and Chrysler, accounted for 95.5 per cent of the industry's output in 1955.[8] While it is generally assumed that the industry is competitive, no study of manufacturers' price policies has been made.

Chartered banks. High concentration in banking is indicated by the fact that there are only nine chartered banks. At the end of 1959, the five largest banks had over 86 per cent of the assets of all banks. Agreements among the banks regarding service charges and so on are well known.

The merger of the Bank of Toronto and the Dominion Bank, and of the Imperial Bank and the Bank of Commerce reduced competition in many areas. There is some doubt whether banking services are covered by the combines legislation, but it is by no means clear that they are not.

Mergers of grocery chains. The *Report of the Royal Commission on Price Spreads of Food Products* (Ottawa, 1959) shows the increase since the end of the war in the percentage of grocery sales concentrated in chain stores and the concentration in the larger chains within the chain store field. Five chains, Dominion, Loblaw, Safeway, A & P, and Steinbergs, accounted for 88 per cent of corporate chain store sales in 1957 (vol. II, p. 34ff., vol. III, p. 99ff.).

Dominion Stores, controlled by the Argus Corporation, acquired Thrift Stores (Montreal) in 1955 and Acadia Stores (Nova Scotia) in 1956. Loblaws, controlled by George Weston Ltd., merged with O.K. Economy Stores (Saskatchewan) in 1958. Steinbergs acquired thirty-eight Grand Union Stores in Ontario, and Ottawa Fruit Supply, a wholesaling firm, in 1959 (vol. II, p. 35).

It is most probable that in the absence of these mergers a greater degree of competition among chain stores would have developed in many localities, since the chains seeking to expand their businesses would have built new stores instead of taking over established outlets.

---

[8] Sun Life Assurance Company, *The Canadian Automotive Industry* (Royal Commission on Canada's Economic Prospects, Ottawa, 1956), p. 50.

APPENDIX II

Estimation of Relative Market Size

Market size is measured in terms of dollars per thousand dollars of Gross National Product. Gross National Product figures are from Dominion Bureau of Statistics: *National Accounts*, 1926-56 and 1958. Sources and methods for the estimates of market size in dollars are given below. All data are for 1956 unless otherwise stated. *Report* means the *Report of the Restrictive Trade Practices Commission* for the year in question. Statistics not obtained from these reports are from publications of the Dominion Bureau of Statistics, unless otherwise stated.

Table VI A

Rubber. Value of output of the industry for 1955.

Electrical wire and cable. Value of output of wire and cable.

Coarse paper, B.C. Value of output of wrapping paper and "Tissue and Other" paper (excluding newsprint and fine papers), multiplied by British Columbia's percentage of Canadian population.

The resulting estimate is very rough. It includes paper going into uses not covered by this case and excludes value added by paper converters.

Wire fencing. Data for 1950 from the report.

Coal, Timmins. Tons of coal sold in Timmins area from the report, p. 10. Average price of $25 per ton based on inspection of price data in the report, p. 17. Data are for 1951.

Asphalt roofing. Value of output of Roofing Paper Industry, 1955.

Transmission and conveyor equipment. Data from the report, appendix, Tables C and D. Figures for 1952. Value of output of all types of equipment listed, by all firms, plus imports.

Coal, Winnipeg. Tons of coal sold, 1950, from the report, p. 25. Price of $25 per ton applied based on data for Timmins area; see above. Resulting estimate is undoubtedly too high since: (1) the report shows a substantial decline in tonnage since 1950; (2) the Timmins prices are probably too high.

Quilting. Value of output of quilts and quilted goods, 1950.

Boxboard. Value of sales of boxboard in Quebec, Ontario, Manitoba, New Brunswick, and Nova Scotia, 1950, estimated by multiplying the cost of materials used by the paper boxes and bags industry in these provinces by the national ratio of costs of paperboard used by the industry to total value of materials used.

Metal culverts. Value of output of sheet metal culvert pipe.

Pulpwood. Value of pulpwood cut on farms, 1950.

Electrical contractors, Ontario. Estimated wholesale sales in Ontario of wiring supplies and other electrical construction materials, apparatus, and equipment by "wholesalers proper," "manufacturers' sales branches," and "agents and brokers" to "industrial and other large users" plus half their sales to retailers, 1951. Sales from *Census of Canada, 1951*, vol. VIII, Table 3. Percentage breakdown of sales by class of customer from Table 8.

The result is likely to be overestimated since sales to "industrial and other large users" include not only sales to contractors but also direct sales to industrial and commercial customers.

Table VI B

Television sets. Only one dealer involved with sales of $50,000 in 1954 (report).

Tobacco. Data for 1955 from the report.

Table VI C

Optical goods. Estimate of total value of retail sales, 1946 (report, p. 13).

Bread. Sales in Alberta, Saskatchewan, and British Columbia, 1946 (report, p. 113).

Flat glass. Very rough estimate, since the domestic output of flat glass is not available. It is estimated as half of the value of output of "pressed, blown and drawn glass." Value of imports is added.

Table VII A

Dental supplies. Sales of dental supplies, 1945 (report, p. 8).

Matches. Data for 1948 (report, p. 10).

Flour milling. Value of shipments of the industry.

Fine papers. Value of output of book and writing paper for 1955.

Gasoline, Vancouver area. Volume of gasoline sales in Vancouver district, 1950 (report, p. 103), multiplied by average of regular and premium prices established by the combine (report, p. 4).

Brewing. Value of production, less taxes.

Sugar. Quantity of sugar sold in three prairie provinces, 1955 (report, pp. 62-7). Average delivered price of $9.30 per 100 lb. in 1956 (report, p. 80) applied to this quantity.

Yeast. Value of shipments of yeast (report, p. 20; D.B.S. data).

Zinc oxide. Value of sales of the three zinc oxide producers (report, pp. 168-70).

Zinc. Value of domestic sales, 1955, estimated from data in the report pp. 138-78. Price of 13.5¢ per lb. applied to domestic sales of 136.8 million lb.

Table VII B

Milk, Vancouver area. Rough estimate of market size based on farm value of fluid milk sales in British Columbia multiplied by proportion of population in Vancouver area.

Fertilizer, eastern Canada. Value of shipments of mixed fertilizer by the fertilizer industry multiplied by ratio of sales (in tons) in eastern Canada to total sold (including exports).

Cigarettes, Toronto. Gross selling value of plant (including duty and sales tax) multiplied by the ratio of the population of metropolitan Toronto to the total for Canada, plus the estimated wholesale and transportation margins.

Electrical equipment. Value of shipments of heavy electrical machinery industry.

Cement. Value of output of cement industry.

Storage batteries. Value of factory shipments of storage batteries.

Molasses. Value of imports of non-edible molasses (Molasses of Cane, n.o.p., tariff item 252) including duty.

Paper bags. Value of output of paper bags in the proper boxes and bags industry multiplied by the ratio of the estimated output of the industry in western Canada to the total.

Telephones, B.C. Gross operating revenue of B.C. Telephone Co.

Table VII C

Agricultural implements. Value of output of industry less value of output of "all other products" produced in the industry.

Electrical apparatus and supplies. Value of output of the "electrical apparatus and supplies" industry group less value of output of the "heavy electrical machinery" industry (included in Table II B) less value of output of electrical wire and cable (included in Table I A).

Primary iron and steel. Value of output of the industry.

Primary non-ferrous metals. Value of output of the smelting and refining industry less value of output of zinc (included in Table III A). Some duplication of values results from the inclusion of transfers from smelters to refineries.

Automobiles. Value of output of the industry.

Chartered banks. The "market" for banks' services is difficult to define. As a lower limit we have used a rough estimate of income originating in the chartered banks. This is taken as the sum of net current operating earnings, remuneration of employees, contributions to pension funds, and depreciation of bank premises. (Data from *Canada Year Book*, 1957-8, p. 1148.)

Mergers, grocery chains. Sales of grocery and combination (grocery and meat) chain stores, 1956, from *Report of Royal Commission on Price Spreads of Food Products*, vol. III, p. 100.

8. The Recent Amendments

THE ANTI-COMBINES MACHINERY we have described was developed by the Liberal party. The Liberal government's legislation of 1951 and 1952 built on foundations established by the Liberal acts and amendments of 1910, 1923, 1937, 1946, and 1949. While the Conservatives supported the major revisions of 1952, they were firmly opposed to the banning of resale price maintenance in 1951.

When Mr. Diefenbaker and his colleagues assumed office, they were reminded of their past statements and promises. They were particularly vulnerable on the issue of resale price maintenance, because they had championed it in the House of Commons in 1951 when the Liberal government sponsored legislation outlawing this practice. The chief spokesman in defence of resale price maintenance had been E. Davie Fulton, later Minister of Justice, responsible for the administration of the Combines Investigation Act. Naturally the advocates of resale price maintenance called on him to remove the ban. The stage was set by letters written to Messrs. Diefenbaker and Fulton on March 30, 1957 (about ten weeks before the election), by Mr. W. A. Gilbert,

General Manager of the Retail Merchants' Association of Canada. In reply, both Conservative leaders pointed to their record as opponents of the ban on resale price maintenance. Mr. Fulton said: ". . . we held the view that the system of price maintenance was one of the greatest protections offered to the small independent merchant and we therefore opposed the government's policy of abandoning this protection"; he concluded with the assurance: ". . . at subsequent sessions we shall be most concerned to see that this problem is faced and adequately dealt with."[1]

During the first months of the new administration, little was heard in Parliament about anti-combines matters except for occasional references to studies being made by Mr. Fulton's advisers of the section of the Combines Investigation Act banning resale price maintenance. Members of the government, of course, received representations from interested parties from time to time. The Distributive Trades Advisory Committee, purporting to speak for fifteen trade associations in the retail, wholesale, and manufacturing field, sought an end to the ban on resale price maintenance and the implementation of a government programme of aid to small business.[2] Its delegation met with the Prime Minister and the Ministers of Justice and of Trade and Commerce on September 5, 1958. The Retail Merchants' Association presented briefs favouring resale price maintenance on September 19, 1957, and November 27, 1958. Submissions were also made by other trade associations and private firms.[3]

When it became generally known that the government was

---

[1] E. D. Fulton to David A. Gilbert, April 18, 1957, quoted in the Submission of the Retail Merchants' Association to David J. Walker, Q.C., Parliamentary Assistant, Department of Justice, Ottawa, September 19, 1957. This brief became part of a large consolidation printed by the Association and distributed to the Conservative caucus on June 17, 1960, prior to Mr. Gilbert's appearance before the Banking and Commerce Committee of the House of Commons to defend the government's proposed amendments to the Combines Investigation Act. It is referred to below as *R.M.A. Consolidation.*

[2] *R.M.A. Consolidation.*

[3] For example, L. W. Prestin of the Sunbeam Corporation of Canada presented a brief, How the Economic Laws of Price Cutting Restrained and Monopolized Trade in Canada, on September 11, 1958. This is reproduced in *R.M.A. Consolidation.*

going to amend the Combines Investigation Act, representations were made by interested parties to the Minister of Justice and the Director of Investigation and Research. While resale price maintenance remained central, other parts of the anti-combines legislation were subjected to criticism. From January 1, 1959, until the first amendments were presented to Parliament in June, the Minister of Justice received submissions from two private firms and five trade associations (one of which sent five separate communications). All but one of the trade associations sought changes in the resale price maintenance section, as did one of the firms. The other firm asked that export trade be exempted from the Combines Investigation Act.[4]

The 1959 Bill

The Minister's proposals to Parliament amounted to a thorough overhaul of the act, and yet they were not presented until very late in the session. There were four major changes. A defence was provided for persons accused of conspiracy under section 32.[5] They had to show that their arrangements did not relate to the fixing of prices, limiting of quantity or quality, dividing markets, restricting channels or methods of distribution, or restricting entry. Six permissible types of co-operation were listed.[6]

[4] Based on a reading of the submissions tabled in the House of Commons by the Solicitor-General on June 8, 1960, in response to a motion for papers by Mr. McIlraith dated May 30, 1960, asking for all submissions.

[5] The reference to section 32 refers to the 1952 act. The government bill also provided for the incorporation of section 411 of the Criminal Code, the section under which most of the prosecutions for conspiracy were initiated.

[6] The new subsection read as follows:

(2) In a prosecution for an offence under subsection (1), it is a defence if the accused

(a) establishes that the conspiracy, combination, agreement or arrangement does not relate in whole or in part to any of the following:
    (i) fixing or enhancing prices,
    (ii) limiting the quantity or quality of production,
    (iii) dividing markets or allocating customers,
    (iv) restricting the channels or methods of distribution,
        or
    (v) restricting entry into a trade or industry, but relates only to
    (vi) the exchange of statistics,
    (vii) the defining of product standards,
    (viii) the exchange of credit information,

Also the accused were required to prove that their arrangements had not operated and were not likely to operate to the "specific detriment" of the public.

Under the new merger provisions, it was a defence if the accused could show that the merger was necessary to achieve economies which would be passed on to the public, and that a substantial degree of competition remained in the industry; moreover, if one of the parties would have been unable to continue operations independently, the merger was to be permitted.

A section on misleading advertising made it an offence to make misleading representations to the public concerning the price at which an article is ordinarily sold. This was intended to deal with catalogue merchants and advertisers who pretended to offer goods at a discount by misrepresenting the usual price as much higher than their actual selling price.

A defence was provided for persons accused of practising resale price maintenance. An accused supplier who had refused to sell to another party in an attempt to dictate resale prices had only to satisfy the court that he "had reason to believe and did believe" that the other party was using the goods as loss-leaders, or was engaging in misleading advertising in respect of the supplier's goods, or was failing to provide service for the goods, or was disparaging the value of the goods. This change would give the supplier more power over the retailer or distributor by making it easier to withhold supplies.[7]

    (ix) definition of trade terms,
     (x) co-operation in research and development,
    (xi) restriction of advertising, or
    (xii) some other matter not enumerated in paragraphs (i) to (v), and
  (b) also establishes that the conspiracy, combination, agreement or arrangement has not operated and is not likely to operate to the specific detriment of the public, whether consumers, producers, or others. (Bill C-59, s. 14.)

[7] There were also other changes which attracted less attention, although some of these were important. A provision was included requiring the Restrictive Trade Practices Commission to find whether a conspiracy relates only to exchanging statistics, defining trade terms and product standards, exchanging credit information, co-operation in research, restriction of advertising, or some other practice not enumerated among the offences in section 32. If the conspiracy relates only to the permitted actions listed, the commission was required to state

Representations Following the Introduction of Bill C-59

The introduction of the proposed amendments led to a flood of representations. These were tabled on June 8, 1960, by the Minister in response to a request from an opposition member. The following observations are based on a reading of this material.

The Minister's material was divided into two sections: "A fair cross-section of comments of a general nature"[8] (consisting of letters from twenty-four individual merchants and consumers) and the main body of submissions. Of the former, twenty-one were from merchants, eighteen of them opposing the ban on resale price maintenance or asking for legislation to curb loss-leader selling. The other three complained of the very large discounts received by large-scale retailers or of the freedom to advertise loss-leaders. The three letters from consumers favoured retaining the ban on resale price maintenance.

The main body of submissions consisted of 143 pieces of correspondence. These may be classified as in Table VIII.

---

its opinion whether the arrangement "has operated or is likely in the foreseeable future to operate to the *specific and substantial detriment of the public*" (Bill C-59, 1959, s. 10; italics supplied). In the cases of mergers and monopolies, the Commission was to find whether the participants acted "with *calculated disregard* for the interests of the public" (*ibid.*; italics supplied).

These changes would involve the Commission in an attempt to measure detriment and appraise intent—both extremely difficult operations.

There was provision for *ad hoc* members of the Commission, "in respect of any matter," to be appointed by the Governor in Council (*ibid.*, s. 7). This would permit additional help to be brought in if the Commission should be overburdened with work, and also permit the addition of persons with particular knowledge or views to the Commission for the consideration of a case.

Courts were permitted to issue restraining orders in cases of conspiracies, and dissolution orders in cases of mergers without a conviction where the offence has been completed (*ibid.*, s. 13).

There were also many verbal changes, mostly occasioned by the consolidation of sections 411 and 412 of the Criminal Code in the Combines Investigation Act. The six persons applying to the director for an investigation were required to present a statement of their evidence. New definitions were supplied.

[8] Quoted from a memorandum attached to the documents tabled by the Minister.

TABLE VIII

INDIVIDUAL PIECES OF CORRESPONDENCE TABLED BY THE MINISTER

	No. of persons or associations	No. of items of correspondence			
		A	B	C	Total
Trade associations	44	82	1		83
Business firms	11	14		3	17
Lawyers on their own account	2	9			9
University economists and political scientists	33		20		20
Canadian Federation of Agriculture	1		3		3
Canadian Association of Consumers	1		3		3
Trade unions and federations	2		2	1	3
The Co-operative Union	1		2		2
Members of Parliament	2			2	2
Canadian Bar Association	1			1	1
TOTAL	98	105	31	7	143

A: Those asking for delay or for changes that would have the effect of weakening the act.

B: Those objecting to the proposed amendment as weakening the act.

C: Not classified.

All but one of the 83 items from trade associations asked for delay or changes that would have the effect of weakening the act. All but 3 of the 17 items from business firms, plus the 9 items from lawyers, took the same position. In other words, 105 out of 145 items favoured delay or amendments likely to weaken the act. On the other hand, all of the 20 items from the university economists objected to the government's proposed changes, as did those from the Canadian Federation of Agriculture, the Canadian Association of Consumers, the Co-operative Union of Canada, 2 of the 3 trade union items and the submission of the Canadian Automotive Trades Association (an organization of service station operators) — or 31 in all.[9] The rest cannot be so classified.

[9] The two items from members of Parliament can be ignored, as they were only covering letters for items from a trade association and a private firm. The item from the Canadian Bar Association can be regarded as neutral because it presents the comments of members of a committee who disagree about some of the issues. One of the trade union submissions is a request for exemption from the act for agreements between fishermen and fish processors.

It is clear, then, that most of the representations were made on behalf of interests which would benefit if the act were made more permissive. The representations from these interested groups were also more persistent. Many of them asked for interviews with the Minister and the Director, whereas none of the academic economists or associations favouring strong anti-combines legislation did so. The former group also appeared to have the assistance of full-time trade association personnel and lawyers, whereas those defending strong anti-combines legislation spoke on their own behalf. Under these conditions the Minister and his officials were exposed to persistent, continuous, and skilful representations mainly from one side. Trade associations, in their briefs, stressed their numerous membership and affiliation and even drafted amendments ready for inclusion in a new bill.

In July 1959, Bill C-59 was withdrawn by the government on the grounds that there was not enough time for a detailed study of the bill before prorogation, and that the government had received "representations from business men and trade associations that the measure should be deferred until they have had an opportunity to study it more thoroughly, and make representations with respect to the combines and merger provisions.[10] It was understood that the government would re-examine its proposals in the light of the representations made, and submit a revised bill the next session. Mr. Howard, the C.C.F. spokesman, requested that the new proposals be introduced early in the next session, and that they go to the Banking and Commerce Committee for exhaustive study.[11]

The 1960 Bill

After considering the numerous suggestions cited above, the government brought down a bill in May 1960 that followed closely the draft of the previous year. It was given first reading on May 6, 1960, and was debated beginning May 30 — fairly near the usual time for prorogation. Mr. Pearson, the leader

---

[10] Statement by Mr. Fulton, July 7, 1959, *House of Commons Debates*, 1959, p. 5577.

[11] *Ibid.*, p. 6404.

of the opposition, and Mr. Howard, the C.C.F. spokesman, made it clear that their parties were opposed to all the important changes involved in the bill. Ten speakers assailed the measure on second reading and three government members spoke in support of the Minister. Then the bill went to the Banking and Commerce Committee for study. The committee met for fifteen days, eleven of which were devoted to hearing and questioning witnesses who appeared voluntarily. Sixteen separate delegations appeared, thirteen consisting of from two to sixteen persons.[12] The positions taken by the witnesses largely paralleled those taken in the submissions relating to the previous year's bill. The spokesmen for the trade associations generally defended the amendments and in some cases asked that additional permissive clauses be inserted in the act. For example, the Fisheries Council of Canada, the Canadian Metal Mining Association, and the Council of the Forest Industries of British Columbia asked that export trade be exempted from the prohibitions of the anti-combines legislation. This request was complied with by a government amendment introduced in the committee stage. All the academic economists and the representatives of the Canadian Association of Consumers and the Canadian Federation of Agriculture were critical of the government's amendments, but were unsuccessful in having their suggestions adopted by the government.[13]

In addition to witnesses and their briefs, the committee re-

---

[12] The organizations represented were: The Distributive Trades Advisory Committee, The Canadian Association of Consumers, The Canadian Electrical Manufacturers' Association, The Canadian Chamber of Commerce, The Fisheries Council of Canada, The Council of the Forest Industries of British Columbia, The Canadian Metal Mining Association, The Canadian Manufacturers' Association, The National Automotive Trades Association, The Board of Trade of Metropolitan Toronto, The Co-operative Union of Canada, The Canadian Federation of Agriculture. In addition, Professors L. A. Skeoch, G. Rosenbluth, and H. E. English (the latter accompanied by two colleagues) presented briefs and answered questions. Maxwell Cohen, Acting Dean of Law at McGill University, addressed the committee and answered questions.

[13] Mr. Hannam of the Canadian Federation of Agriculture accepted the consolidation of the relevant sections of the Criminal Code in the Combines Investigation Act, but was critical of the amendments affecting resale price maintenance and conspiracy (Standing Committee on Banking and Commerce, *Minutes of Proceedings and Evidence*, House of Commons, 1960, pp. 596-7).

ceived eighteen written submissions. Six were from persons and firms in the photographic products retailing trade asking for controls against loss-leader selling. One from a firm selling auto parts took a similar position. Six others were from trade associations and business firms, seeking more permissive amendments to the act. An amendment obliging promotional allowances to be granted on a basis proportional to volume of sales was criticized by four of them. The other five letters were critical of the government's bill.[14] The Committee proceedings served to show up the alignment of business interests behind the government's proposed changes and the opposition of academic economists and organized agricultural, co-operative, and consumer interests.[15]

When the bill went to the committee of the whole house, it was vigorously debated. The C.C.F. proposed eleven amendments and the Liberals nine, but the measure emerged with no substantial alteration of its major proposals, except for the amendment exempting agreements relating to export trade.[16] In third reading, a further three amendments, two C.C.F. and one Liberal, to defeat the bill or refer it back to committee were voted down and the bill passed. It passed through the Senate in three days, encountering vigorous Liberal opposition the first day, but this was not sustained.[17]

The Act As Amended

Instead of the general prohibition of restraints on competition

---

[14] They consisted of: one from a consumer asking that the ban on resale price maintenance be retained, one from G. E. Britnell, Head of the Economics Department at the University of Saskatchewan, enclosing a brief from five members of his department criticizing the government's amendments, one from Professor H. E. English of Carleton University providing documentation for a point raised when he appeared before the committee, one from a member of the committee presenting further arguments from the President of the Canadian Association of Consumers, and one from the Canadian Bar Association criticizing several points in the bill.

[15] The National Automotive Trades Association, an organization of service station lessees, also opposed the government's proposals.

[16] The amendments that were accepted and the debate about them will be found in *House of Commons Debates,* 1960, pp. 6918, 6943, 6966, 7000, 7004, and *passim.*

[17] *Senate Debates,* 1960, pp. 1145, 1162-89, 1190, 1195-7.

which are "undue" or "to the detriment of the public," the act now specifies that a "conspiracy, combination, agreement, or arrangement" is illegal only if it lessens competition unduly "in respect of one of the following": prices, quantity or quality, markets or customers, channels or methods of distribution, or entry and expansion of rival firms. The act, moreover, lists areas in which agreements and so forth are specifically declared legal (provided, of course, that they do not also invade the prohibited area of prices, quantity or quality, and so on). These include the exchange of statistics, definition of product standards, the restriction of advertising, and others.[18]

It is not easy to predict how the courts will interpret this change in the legislation. The Minister has argued that it merely clarifies the existing legal situation,[19] but it is clear that if there is any change, it must be in the direction of making the act more permissive and making it more difficult to obtain a conviction where agreements with anti-competitive effects exist. The change in wording may render the courts more receptive to the suggestion, always advanced by defence counsel, that "specific detriment" must be established in each case. Moreover, the new wording provides "psychological encouragement" to businessmen to make agreements and arrangements that tend to "infringe competition."[20]

In line with the change in legislation regarding agreements, the Commission is required to find whether the agreement relates only to the permitted practices (exchanging statistics, etc.), and if so, whether it is likely to lessen competition unduly in any of the specified respects (prices, markets, etc.).[21]

The prohibition of resale price maintenance was greatly weakened. A supplier, accused of refusal to supply a dealer, can escape conviction if he "satisfies the court that he and anyone upon whose report he depended had reasonable cause to believe and

---

[18] Office Consolidation, Combines Investigation Act, R.S.C. 1952, c. 314, as amended by 1953-54, c. 51, 1960, c. 45, s. 32.

[19] *House of Commons Debates*, 1960, p. 4339 ff.

[20] See the testimony of Maxwell Cohen before the Banking and Commerce Committee of the House of Commons (*Minutes of Proceedings and Evidence*, no. 9, 1960), pp. 556-7.

[21] Combines Investigation Act, s. 19(1a).

did believe" that the dealer concerned was using the article for purposes of advertising, or to attract customers, instead of making a profit on it, that he engaged in misleading advertising, or that he did not provide adequate servicing.[22] These defences are so broad that a successful prosecution for resale price maintenance is hard to imagine.

An amendment that was added to Bill C-58 at its third reading exempts combinations, agreements, and so forth, relating "only to the export of articles from Canada," provided they do not reduce the volume of exports, restrain the export business of a non-member, or lessen domestic competition "unduly."[23]

The prohibition of price discrimination was left unenforceable; that is to say, price discrimination is banned only when it relates to sales "of like quality and quantity." A clause was added, however, requiring that "promotional allowances" and similar concessions "not applied directly to the selling price" be granted to all customers on a basis proportional to their purchases, if they are granted to any.[24]

Less drastic changes in the act include the following:

A new clause prohibits misleading advertising about the price at which goods are ordinarily sold.[25] This was intended to deal with catalogue merchants and others who misrepresent the "regular" price as being well above their actual price.

The section permitting the reduction of customs duties on a product that is the subject of a conspiracy was changed to permit such reduction only in cases where the "disadvantage to the public is *presently being* facilitated" by the duties.[26] This would permit the parties to a conspiracy to desist, and by so doing, save their tariff protection.

An option was granted to the Crown to proceed by "information" as well as by prosecution. This involves a restraining order but no conviction and no penalty. A new provision permitted the court, in proceedings commenced by information, to issue

---

[22] *Ibid.*, s. 34(5).
[23] S. 32(4) and (5).
[24] S. 33B.
[25] S. 33C.
[26] S. 29. Our italics.

restraining orders or orders to dissolve a merger or monopoly without a conviction being secured. The Exchequer Court was granted jurisdiction in combines cases, but only with the consent of the accused.[27]

The wording of the amendments suggests that the rules against agreements and against resale price maintenance have been seriously impaired, at the same time that the chances of proceeding against mergers have been greatly weakened by judicial decisions.[28] What the amendments mean in practice, however, will only be discovered as the administrative record is built up, and as the new clauses are subjected to judicial interpretation.

The Conservative government's sensitivity to the requests of business lobbies in this case contrasts with the situation in 1951, when the Liberal government passed the ban on resale price maintenance over the protests of business groups. As we have shown in chapter IX, there are good reasons for the view that the Liberal government's action was dictated in part by the need for some striking measure that could be represented as combating inflation, which was a major political problem at the time. Moreover, the Liberal government in 1951 must have been concerned to wipe out the impression (which had been fostered by the opposition's exploitation of the flour milling incident) that it was in favour of combines. It is also relevant that in 1951 the authoritative opinions of the Royal Commission on Prices, the MacQuarrie Committee, and Mr. McGregor, the recently resigned Combines Commissioner, could be cited in support of the ban on resale price maintenance,[29] while in 1960 there were no such independent "official" authorities opposed to the government's amendments.

[27] Ss. 40, 31, 41A.
[28] The Beer and Sugar cases. See appendices I and II to chapter VII.
[29] *Report of the Royal Commission on Prices* (Ottawa, 1949), vol. I, pp. 27-8, 41.

9. Summary and Conclusions

The Combines Investigation Act furnishes an excellent example of the kind of political tight-rope walking that is necessary in a modern industrial democracy. Governments try hard to avoid antagonizing large blocks of voters, and at the same time to maintain the support of substantial business interests, not only because political campaigns are expensive, but also because, in a multitude of ways, the environment in which government operates is influenced by the actions and attitudes of the major business groups. Very often, particularly in non-economic areas, there is no conflict between these objectives, and, even in the economic field, important aspects of government policy may not involve conflict. Everybody favours prosperity. Where conflict arises between the interests of these two elements, the government is compelled to work out a "compromise"; the effect of such a policy on the public interest can only be ascertained by the study of particular examples.

Anti-combines policy is an instance of this kind of conflict. One has only to read the Combines Investigation Act (in any of its versions since 1923) to realize that it is bound to arouse the opposition of major business groups, while it will appeal to the mass of farmers and employees and to individual businessmen, particularly small businessmen, who are the victims of monopolistic restrictions.

In a period of general prosperity, the damage to the public interest arising from monopolistic structures and practices is generalized and not felt acutely by any one section of the population. The economic inefficiencies in the production and allocation of goods introduced by monopoly reduce the real national output, but other forces are pushing it up. The transfer of income to the monopolistic groups is hidden by the general rise in incomes. It follows that there is no significant political group that has any strong interest in checking the effectiveness with which combines legislation is enforced. Political leaders find, therefore, that the interest of the mass of voters in combines legislation is satisfied by action which is symbolic and dramatic, though it may not be particularly effective.

In such a situation, the compromise between the requirements of mass support and the requirements of business support is likely to take the form of limited enforcement activity with the emphasis on a few flagrant cases of price agreements which will produce spectacular judicial decisions. This leaves the activities of the leading corporations substantially untouched.

There is one qualification, however. When general prosperity is accompanied by inflation, the attention of the public turns to the determinants of prices at the retail level. In such a situation, a government may attempt to reduce public criticism of its policies by directing the attention of the public to monopolistic arrangements, particularly at the retail level.

These general considerations help to explain the revision of the combines machinery and the selective implementation of the recommendations of the MacQuarrie Committee. Under the St. Laurent–Howe administration, the backgrounds and personalities of the government leaders, their natural desire for financial support from business interests for campaign purposes, the remoteness from the electorate caused by the duration of the Liberal regime, and the general economic prosperity all favoured a certain solicitude for the interests of large corporations. In the field of combines legislation, the logical development of government policy would have been towards reduction in emphasis upon activities that might disturb major business groups.

The administrative structure under the Combines Investigation Act was, however, such that the activities of the commissioner could not be controlled by the government, and he did, in fact, follow a policy that was the direct opposite of that suggested by the considerations above. His twenty pre-war reports had dealt mainly with small business: retailers of coal, wholesalers of fruit and vegetables, bakers, building contractors, manufacturers of fruit baskets, and so on. After the war, however, he launched investigations into international cartels, the pulp and paper industry, the rubber industry, wire and cable, matches, flat glass, and so forth. Large manufacturing corporations were therefore attacked, and in many cases large international interests were involved. Seen in this context, the dispute over the flour milling report was clearly the last straw. In view of the conflict between the Commissioner's policy and that of the government, it was desirable from the government's point of view that the Commissioner should resign. It was also desirable that the administrative structure should be altered in such a way as to reduce the independent power of the commissioner. Business interests had always urged that the commissioner should not combine the powers of "judge and prosecutor," and the government was now extremely receptive to this idea. The change of personnel was therefore followed by the splitting up of the functions of the commissioner, as recommended by the MacQuarrie Committee. However, most of the MacQuarrie Committee's recommendations, which might have led to more effective action against the monopolistic tendencies of large corporations, were rejected. These included the recommendation of large-scale research into problems of industrial organization and monopoly, the search for more effective remedies than criminal prosecution, and the integration of other aspects of government policy with combines policy.

How does the prohibition of resale price maintenance fit into this picture? Such a ban had long been advocated by the Commissioner, and the Royal Commission on Prices in 1949 made a similar recommendation.[1] The government does not appear to have developed a strong interest in this issue until 1951, when it asked the MacQuarrie Committee to submit its views on resale price maintenance "at an early date."[2] It is probable that inflation caused by the Korean war was a major factor in the government's sudden sponsorship of this cause. It was politically important that the government take some action against high retail prices, and the ban on resale price maintenance was a dramatic move of this kind. It did not, of course, deal with the basic inflationary forces, but in the political arena it could be represented as a move against inflation.[3] It is also significant that resale price maintenance has not in general been strongly supported by large manufacturing interests, but rather by small retailers and other distributors.

The administration of the Combines Investigation Act since 1952 has on the whole followed the lines of the foregoing analysis. With the new administrative structure, the staff was considerably increased, but since then it has not kept pace with the growth of the economy. The proceedings against major manufacturing groups, planned and launched by the preceding Commissioner,

[1] *Report of the Royal Commission on Prices* (Ottawa, 1949), vol. I, pp. 27-8, 41; vol. II, pp. 238-9, 256-9.

[2] MacQuarrie *Report*, p. 55.

[3] In public discussion preceding the legislation, the contemplated ban on resale price maintenance was generally linked with the inflationary situation. Thus a *Financial Post* editorial on October 13, 1951, stated: "The government's avowed intention of legislating on resale price maintenance is not impressive. It's true that the high cost of living is the problem uppermost in the popular mind. But it looks very much as if the government is going to make a big show of 'doing something' about the high cost of living by tilting against resale price agreements."

In the House of Commons, Mr. St. Laurent linked the ban on resale price maintenance with the inflation, while at the same time suggesting that it was not likely to have much effect as an anti-inflationary move: "As regards immediate additional measures to curb inflation ... the only one we are prepared to submit at this time is the one that will arise out of this report of the combines committee with respect to resale prices. I do not think that is going to have a very substantial effect on the index of the cost of living; I think it is apt to bring about some change in resale prices, because I do know that there are some instances where the spread between what the consumer has to pay and what goes to the primary producer seems to be inordinately large." (*House of Commons Debates,* 1951, Second Session, pp. 41-2.)

have not been dropped, but most of the new cases have been price agreements involving small or medium-sized firms. Monopolistic situations that have not been investigated or whose investigations have been dropped at an early stage have remained large in comparison with those that have been effectually dealt with. A few merger cases have been investigated, but only two, the Canadian Breweries and Western Sugar cases, have been tested in court. In both cases the government failed to secure convictions, and the judicial interpretations suggest that a merger can be attacked under the legislation only if it eliminates virtually all competition. The government has not appealed these judgements.[4] There has thus been no effective action in relation to mergers. Nor has there been any serious attempt to deal with the problem of discrimination, except for the new provision relating to promotional allowances.

The trend in administrative policy is also evident in what may be considered more minor aspects of administration. The colour and layout of the covers of the published reports have been changed so as to make them even less attractive than they were before, and press releases have been reduced to the point where they reveal nothing of the contents of the reports. Thus Mackenzie King's policy of using publicity, or the threat of publicity, as a deterrent, has been quietly abandoned in favour of a policy of minimizing embarrassment to the parties concerned.

The amendments of 1960 represent a further step in the direction of minimizing interference with monopolistic business structures and practices. The ban on resale price maintenance has not been removed, but has probably been rendered virtually unenforceable. The change in the wording regarding price agreements has undermined the doctrine that they are illegal *per se* and has provided psychological encouragement for agreements that take the form of a concern with statistics, product standards, and so on. Price agreements in the export field have been explicitly permitted.

We have suggested that the ineffective administration of the

---

[4] The wording has been changed slightly in the 1960 amendments, but the change is not such as to invalidate the judicial interpretations. The government's decision not to appeal the Sugar case was announced on January 27, 1961.

Combines Investigation Act is an aspect of the compromise between the power of the vote and the power of the dollar that is a feature of Canadian democracy. This does not mean, however, that the government and the civil servants who administer the act are engaged in a conspiracy to fool the public. On the contrary, the evidence suggests that the staff of both branches of the combines machinery are conscientious and hard-working. To some extent, of course, ineffective administration is the result of inadequate budgets and inadequate staffing. But on the whole, neither the director nor successive ministers appear to have been conscious of any substantial inadequacies in the size of the staff. Their conception of the combines problem and of the role of the combines machinery has made them unaware of any serious inadequacy.

The administration's view of the proper role of the combines machinery has been described as a "cops and robbers" concept. Combines officers are viewed as a species of specialized policemen who enforce a particular statute by looking for violators, investigating their activities, and bringing them to justice before the courts. For this kind of job, competent investigators and lawyers are needed. Other types of personnel, for example, research economists, are merely "frills." The branch seems to estimate its success by its record of convictions. The professional staff of the combines branch comes by this view naturally since its leading members are lawyers. For the Cabinet ministers who have appointed the key personnel of the combines branch, this is also a natural view since any other, such as that put forward by the MacQuarrie Committee, would render the necessary political compromise more difficult.

The "cops and robbers" attitude has led to concentration on the investigation of a particular kind of case: *per se* offences, especially price-fixing conspiracies. These were cases in which the law was clear and the job of the director was simply to collect evidence.[5] Evidence that will stand up in court is not always easy to obtain. If the price agreement involves only a small

---

[5] Our comments on the conduct of operations under the act apply to the situation preceding the 1960 amendments. In particular, the statement that "the law is clear" no longer applies.

number of firms, it is probable that no documentary evidence exists. This had led to the dropping of some cases where other indications pointed to serious infractions of the act. Some, at least, of these cases have involved very large firms, such as the producers of heavy electrical equipment. However, when the price fixing agreement involves a very large number of firms, it is more likely that written records will have to be kept. These cases are therefore more likely to be prosecuted. They also tend to involve medium-sized or small firms rather than the largest corporate giants. No serious attempt has been made to adapt the combines machinery to cope with this problem.

Concentration on the goal of successful prosecution also meant that cases where the application of the law was doubtful were not developed. Thus the courts were not given a chance to clarify the meaning of all sections of the act, and the act was not given its full application. Price agreements were generally prosecuted under the Criminal Code and their status under section 32 of the Combines Act was not clarified.[6] The application of the law to mergers was tested only at the end of the period under review and the clause on price discrimination remains unexplored.

Neglect of the research function is also a consequence of the "cops and robbers" attitude. Instead of the establishment of a research division, as recommended by the MacQuarrie Committee, only one senior research officer was appointed in 1951, and no further research staff was added. This research officer subsequently left the branch and has not yet been replaced, so that for all practical purposes no specialist research personnel were

---

[6] The Director's annual reports stress the point that "a recent case, under the Act, in the British Columbia Court of Appeal" suggests that conviction under section 32 of the Combines Act requires "proof of some immediate and specific harm" instead of the rule established under the Criminal Code cases, that price agreements are illegal *per se* (*Annual Reports*, 1958 and 1959, p. 8). Yet the government, although given an opportunity for a new trial of this case (Vancouver Gasoline) decided to drop it (see appendix II).

[7] The Director's *Annual Report* for the year ended March 31, 1961, states that the Combines Branch was reorganized as of that date, and that a Research Section was established, the functions of which are described as the planning of research inquiries, liaison with other government departments, and the study of anti-trust practices in the international field. There is also a new Merger Section for the investigation of mergers and monopolies (pp. 42-43).

employed at the end of our period.[7] Owing to the neglect of research, no body of knowledge has been built up about the structure of industry in Canada to form the basis for policy-making in the combines field.

The problem of the legalistic orientation of senior combines personnel and the neglect of research, has been compounded because conviction in a court of law has been the only remedy employed. Thus the evidence collected is the type to which courts are accustomed. The practice of turning prosecutions over to lawyers in private practice has emphasized the legalistic bias, which avoids cases involving monopoly, merger, and price discrimination, where economic analysis is essential.

The neglect of the research function in the office of the Director of Investigation and Research has apparently been accompanied by a similar neglect on the part of the Restrictive Trade Practices Commission. The time of the Commission has been largely taken up in acting as a sort of court of first instance, reviewing the factual evidence presented by the director in price agreement cases, and presenting it to the minister and the public in a lengthy report. Curiously enough, the Commission has adopted the practice of avoiding specific recommendations to the minister about prosecution. As a result, it is not clear exactly what contribution the Commission makes to the consideration of *per se* cases.

In the few cases involving merger or price discrimination, the Commission's discussions have been narrow and legalistic and have not adequately explored the basic economic issues. Like a court, it has generally confined itself to the consideration of the evidence presented by the director and the opposing parties.

Our objective here has been analysis, not prescription. Certain recommendations for legislative and administrative changes, however, follow fairly clearly from our review and are summarized below. They are based on the assumption that the "cops and robbers" concept of combines administration is mistaken. In the Canadian economy, monopolistic practices are not the infrequent acts of a criminal minority. Monopolistic market structures and practices are widespread and constitute the typical business environment. We believe that these elements of monopoly seriously impair the economic and social health of the country, and that combines legislation should be effective and should be enforced.

Clearly the MacQuarrie Committee's recommendation that a research organization be set up should be implemented. The simplest way would be to establish two divisions under the director, one to conduct investigations (as at present) and the other a new research division. The latter, under an experienced research economist, should have *carte blanche* to study any aspect of the structure and functioning of business firms and industries, and it should prepare reports on its findings. It would have to be given the power to examine the records of firms and to require that they provide information as directed. Only with such powers can the actual conditions of business in Canada become known. Such information is essential if the government is to frame appropriate and effective legislation. Indeed, the research division could be asked for studies of areas in which the government is contemplating legislative or administrative changes. Naturally this would include such beclouded areas as merger, monopoly, and price discrimination.

The almost exclusive reliance on the criminal law is a serious shortcoming of Canadian anti-combines methods. Other remedies, such as legislation under the federal "trade and commerce" power, should be explored. The 1960 amendments, providing for a court order to dissolve a merger or monopoly without a conviction, providing for the institution of proceedings by "information" as well as by prosecution, and providing for cases to be heard in the Exchequer Court are examples of more direct effective remedies.[8]

Modification of tariff or patent protection in order to promote competition is provided for in the act, but these provisions have hardly ever been used. The MacQuarrie Committee recommended that the act be amended so that such action would not have to wait on a finding that a combine exists, but could be taken whenever "the requirements of the public interest" made

---

[8] The provision for cases to be heard by the Exchequer Court is greatly weakened by the proviso that no case can be tried there without the consent of the accused.

it desirable.[9] This recommendation was never implemented, but the change should be made and the government's power over tariffs and patents should be used to promote competition.

More generally, as the MacQuarrie Committee pointed out, the interaction between combines administration and other aspects of government policy should be constantly kept in mind by governments at all levels, and possible effects on competitive conditions should be considered in planning and administering government policy in various fields. For example, some aspects of the tax structure may promote mergers and concentration, while others may encourage the formation of new firms. Procurement by competitive tender will encourage competition and give a fair chance to aggressive small firms. Procurement by negotiated deals will usually benefit the larger firms, regardless of efficiency, and promote concentration. The promotion of low interest rates by the Bank of Canada and the provision of credit through such agencies as Central Mortgage and Housing and the Industrial Development Bank will tend to encourage new businesses and small firms, while a "tight money" policy and restriction of government credit will tend to favour large firms with adequate internal sources of finance. Government trade promotion policies and government research activities, and the manner in which research results are made available to business, government licence policies (for instance, for television stations) and resource development policies, all these have important implications for competition, particularly in new industries.

The administrative arrangements currently employed in combines cases could be improved. The Commission normally considers all cases before they go to court. Since most are routine price fixing conspiracies, there is really nothing to be gained by the Commission's review, and the accused businessmen are understandably disturbed at having their arrangements and practices reported in public before an action has been brought in the courts. Such routine cases should go directly to the courts for disposal. The Commission would then be free to examine in detail those cases in which the elucidation of the public interest is more complex; and if its staff were increased by the addition

[9] MacQuarrie *Report*, pp. 41-2.

of research personnel, it could develop an approach to these neglected areas of the combines problem by hearing and reporting on such cases.

The Commission's reports should contain specific recommendations relating to prosecution, and should discuss fully the policy issues involved. This would help to take the decision regarding prosecution out of politics, as the minister would be inclined to follow the Commission's recommendation. If he chose to reject it, he would have to satisfy Parliament that he had legitimate reasons for so doing. The minister would thus be relieved of pressure from the private interests involved, and, by making his action formal only, provide both the appearance and probably the substance of greater impartiality.

Our main plea is for a change in the approach of the responsible authorities to the problem of combines. We must escape from the "cops and robbers" concept.

www.ingramcontent.com/pod-product-compliance
Lightning Source LLC
Chambersburg PA
CBHW031350060726
47590CB00007B/2706